COSORI Air Fryer Cookbook for Beginners

1200 Days Easy, Quick and Fresh Air Fryer
Recipes to Make Most of Your COSORI Air Fryer

Milan Helms

Disclaimer Notice:

Please note the information contained within this document is for educational and entertainment purposes only. All effort has been executed to present accurate, up to date, reliable, complete information. No warranties of any kind are declared or implied. Readers acknowledge that the author is not engaged in the rendering of legal, financial, medical or professional advice. The content within this book has been derived from various sources. Please consult a licensed professional before attempting any techniques outlined in this book.

By reading this document, the reader agrees that under no circumstances is the author responsible for any losses, direct or indirect, that are incurred as a result of the use of the information contained within this document, including, but not limited to, errors, omissions, or inaccuracies.

CONTENT

Introduction

I love to prepare healthy and sumptuous meal for my friends and family. That is why I use the Cosori Air Fryer. Do you know that with little or no oil needed, I am able to cook my food on average 85% less fat using the Cosori Air fryer which is better than the deep-fried food? My Cosori Air Fryer has thirteen cooking functions. That gives me the freedom to adjust and save any preset I prefer. I enjoy all the tastiness of my fried food no minding the impact on my health. An air fryer is a counter top kitchen appliance that cooks the same way a convection oven will. Nevertheless, I prefer it to the convection oven. This is because it works faster.

The Cosori Air Fryer is especially reputable for being able to your cook food to deep fried crispy perfection with little or no oil. It makes use of the speedy air and heat circulation technology to work effectively. Nutritionist and several health experts have discovered that air fried foods are healthier than deep fried foods. This is because it reduces calories up to twenty six percent. This way, it makes it a healthier alternative for cooking particularly for persons having cholesterol problems.

If you do not know whether or not to buy the Cosori Air Fryer, you need to read all the details I have compiled for you. I believe this will convince you more as to why the Cosori Air fryer is an excellent kitchen requirement.

It cooks my meal to crispy perfection. I love the well aerated inner basket that comes with it as well as the square basket which has more than round baskets. With the Cosori Air Fryer, I am able to cook my food in a shorter time than using the conventional oven.

Cosori Air Fryer Parts and Functions

I strongly believe that there is no doubt about the capacity and usefulness of the Cosori Air Fryer. It helps to make the process of my air frying easy than normal. During my research, I discovered that the effectiveness of the Cosori Air Fryer lies in its different functions and parts. So, I will be sharing with you what you should know about the different parts of the Cosori Air Fryer and what they do.

Different Parts and Their Functions

The Cosori Air Fryer is made up of various parts and these parts perform different functions. You need to know these parts before you can know how they work.

1. The control panel regulates the functionality of the Cosori Air Fryer and is where most of the operation takes place.

2. The 13 one-touch cooking functions and rapid 360° air circulation helps to give a crispier outcome when you use less oil. Do you know that you can select your preferred preset with one simple tap whenever you want to cook? You can also set temperature and cook time for personal recipes.
3. The air fryer comes with a 5.8-quart square basket that is very spacious.
4. I love the digital screen in the Cosori Air Fryer, which makes it a great alternative than their regular air fryers that comes with a dial knob and can easily get damaged.
5. My Cosori Air Fryer comes with a shake reminder which beeps to alert you to shake the basket whenever you are making use of the preset for fries.

How to use the Cosori Air Fryer

If you do not know how to use the Cosori Air Fryer, you may not be able to get the best out of it.

1. Take away every sticker and packaging from the air fryer.
2. Position the air fryer on a balanced heat resistant surface with sufficient room on every sides
3. You must ensure that you read the product manual well. This is because different brands work differently. It will also help you to recognize the different components of your air fryer.
4. You have to firstly insert the air fryer cord into an electric power outlet before you start using it.
5. Ideally the Cosori Air Fryer comes with two baskets; the inner and the outer basket. Never press the basket release button while carrying the baskets. Instead, Only separate the baskets to clean or after cooking, with the baskets resting flat on a counter, or any level, heat-resistant surface.
6. You must make sure that you wash the air fryer basket and dry it.
7. You have to firstly insert the air fryer cord into an electric power outlet before you start using it

Benefits of Using the Cosori Air Fryer

There are many reasons why I consider the Cosori Air Fryer as one of my favorite cooking tools.

1. Less Oil

The air fryer makes use of about eighty five percent less oil than the regular deep-frying methods while preserving the sumptuous taste, making it a great delicacy for families and friends.

2. Convenient Design

The air fryer gives a crispy outcome in less time than the regular oven. The design makes it very convenient to use. My Cosori Air Fryer has a flat perforated design.

3. Easy to clean

The baskets are very simple to clean whether with your hands or with a dishwasher. This is owing to the fact that it comes with no ridges. The exterior part of my Cosori Air Fryer is resistant to stain.

4. Warranty

My Cosori Air Fryer has a year warranty and I can even increase it to two years when you register virtually within fourteen days of purchase. In fact, even if it exceeds two weeks of purchase, you can still get a warranty. This is because I was still able to register my product even after 30 days of purchase and still got my warranty extended.

5. Automatic pause and resume.

I was amazed to discover that whenever I pulled out the basket during cooking, my air fryer pauses automatically and resumes immediately I push it back inside.

Safety Precaution and Cleaning Tips

There are safety precautions that you must know whenever you are making use of the Cosori Air Fryer. There are also important cleaning and maintenance tips that you must always take note whenever you are using the Cosori Air Fryer.

1. You must make sure that you do not deep or soak the air fryer housing or plug in liquid or water.
2. Whenever you are making use of the Cosori Air fryer, ensure that do not watch your children move near your air fryer.
3. Whenever you are not making use of your Cosori Air Fryer, unplug it and before cleaning, make sure that you give it enough time to cool before taking off the components.
4. If your air fryer is spoilt or if the cord or plug is damaged, do not use anymore or contact customer support service.
5. On no account must you make use of any third-party replacement component or accessories, as this may lead to injuries.
6. You must never position your air fryer or any of its component on a stove, near gas or electric burners, or in a heated oven.
7. If your air fryer has hot liquid or hot oil in it, you must be very careful when moving your air fryer or removing the baskets.
8. You must not use metal scouring pads to clean your air fryer. This is because metal compartments can break off the pad. It can cause electric shock whenever it touches any electrical parts.
9. Do not place anything on top of your air fryer. Do not store anything inside your air fryer.

Chapter 1   Breakfasts

Coconut Brown Rice Porridge with Dates

Prep time: 10 minutes | Cook time: 23 minutes | Serves 1 to 2

1 cup canned coconut milk
½ cup cooked brown rice
¼ cup unsweetened shredded coconut
¼ cup packed dark brown sugar

½ teaspoon kosher salt
¼ teaspoon ground cardamom
4 large Medjool dates, pitted and roughly chopped
Heavy cream, for serving (optional)

1. Select Preheat, adjust the temperature to 375°F (191°C), set time to 23 minutes and press Start/Pause. 2. In a baking pan, stir together the coconut milk, rice, shredded coconut, brown sugar, salt, cardamom, and dates. 3. Once preheated, place the pan into preheated basket. Stirring halfway through. 4. Remove the pan from the air fryer and divide the porridge among bowls. Drizzle the porridge with cream, if you like, and serve hot.

Cinnamon-Raisin Bagels

Prep time: 30 minutes | Cook time: 10 minutes | Makes 4 bagels

Oil, for spraying
¼ cup raisins
1 cup self-rising flour, plus more for dusting

1 cup plain Greek yogurt
1 teaspoon ground cinnamon
1 large egg

1. Line the air fryer basket with parchment and spray lightly with oil. 2. Place the raisins in a bowl of hot water and let sit for 10 to 15 minutes, until they have plumped. This will make them extra juicy. 3. Select Preheat, adjust the temperature to 350°F (177°C), set time to 10 and press Start/Pause. 4. In a large bowl, mix together the flour, yogurt, and cinnamon with your hands or a large silicone spatula until a ball is formed. It will be quite sticky for a while. 5. Drain the raisins and gently work them into the ball of dough. 6. Place the dough on a lightly floured work surface and divide into 4 equal pieces. Roll each piece into an 8- or 9-inch-long rope and shape it into a circle, pinching the ends together to seal. 7. In a small bowl, whisk the egg. Brush the egg onto the tops of the dough. 8. Once preheated, place the dough in the prepared basket and cook. 9. Serve immediately.

Cheesy Cauliflower "Hash Browns"

Prep time: 30 minutes | Cook time: 24 minutes | Makes 6 hash browns

2 ounces (57 g) 100% cheese crisps
1 (12-ounce / 340-g) steamer bag cauliflower, cooked according to package instructions

1 large egg
½ cup shredded sharp Cheddar cheese
½ teaspoon salt

1. Let cooked cauliflower cool 10 minutes. 2. Select Preheat, adjust the temperature to 375°F (191°C), set time to 12 and press Start/Pause. 3. Place cheese crisps into food processor and pulse on low 30 seconds until crisps are finely ground. 4. Using a kitchen towel, wring out excess moisture from cauliflower and place into food processor. 5. Add egg to food processor and sprinkle with Cheddar and salt. Pulse five times until mixture is mostly smooth. 6. Cut two pieces of parchment to fit air fryer basket. Separate mixture into six even scoops and place three on each piece of ungreased parchment, keeping at least 2 inch of space between each scoop. Press each into a hash brown shape, about ¼ inch thick. 7. Once preheated, place one batch on parchment into air fryer basket. Turning hash browns halfway through cooking. Hash browns will be golden brown when done. Repeat with second batch. 8. Allow 5 minutes to cool. Serve warm.

Parmesan Sausage Egg Muffins

Prep time: 5 minutes | Cook time: 20 minutes | Serves 4

6 ounces (170 g) Italian sausage, sliced
6 eggs
⅛ cup heavy cream

Salt and ground black pepper, to taste
3 ounces (85 g) Parmesan cheese, grated

1. Select Preheat, adjust the temperature to 350ºF (177ºC), set time to 20 minutes and press Start/Pause. Grease a muffin pan. 2. Put the sliced sausage in the muffin pan. 3. Beat the eggs with the cream in a bowl and season with salt and pepper. 4. Pour half of the mixture over the sausages in the pan. 5. Sprinkle with cheese and the remaining egg mixture. 6. Once preheated, place the pan into air fryer basket, and cook. 7. Serve immediately.

Turkey Sausage Breakfast Pizza

Prep time: 15 minutes | Cook time: 24 minutes | Serves 2

4 large eggs, divided
1 tablespoon water
½ teaspoon garlic powder
½ teaspoon onion powder
½ teaspoon dried oregano
2 tablespoons coconut flour

3 tablespoons grated Parmesan cheese
½ cup shredded provolone cheese
1 link cooked turkey sausage, chopped (about 2 ounces / 57 g)
2 sun-dried tomatoes, finely chopped
2 scallions, thinly sliced

1. Select Preheat, adjust the temperature to 400ºF (204ºC), set time to 10 minutes and press Start/Pause. Line a cake pan with parchment paper and lightly coat the paper with olive oil. 2. In a large bowl, whisk 2 of the eggs with the water, garlic powder, onion powder, and dried oregano. Add the coconut flour, breaking up any lumps with your hands as you add it to the bowl. Stir the coconut flour into the egg mixture, mixing until smooth. Stir in the Parmesan cheese. Allow the mixture to rest for a few minutes until thick and dough-like. 3. Transfer the mixture to the prepared pan. Use a spatula to spread it evenly and slightly up the sides of the pan. Top with the cheeses, sausage, and sun-dried tomatoes. 4. Once preheated, place the pan into the air fryer basket and cook until the crust is set but still light in color. 5. Break the remaining 2 eggs into a small bowl, then slide them onto the pizza. Return the pizza to the air fryer. Cook for 10 to 14 minutes or until the egg whites are set and the yolks are the desired doneness. Top with the scallions and allow to rest for 5 minutes before serving.

Cornflakes Toast Sticks

Prep time: 10 minutes | Cook time: 6 minutes | Serves 4

2 eggs
½ cup milk
⅛ teaspoon salt
½ teaspoon pure vanilla extract

¾ cup crushed cornflakes
6 slices sandwich bread, each slice cut into 4 strips
Maple syrup, for dipping
Cooking spray

1. Select Preheat, adjust the temperature to 390ºF (199ºC) and press Start/Pause. Line a baking pan that fits into your air fryer with parchment paper.2. In a small bowl, beat together the eggs, milk, salt, and vanilla. 3. Put crushed cornflakes on a plate or in a shallow dish. 4. Dip bread strips in egg mixture, shake off excess, and roll in cornflake crumbs. 5. Spray both sides of bread strips with oil and put on the parchment paper. 6. Once preheated, put baking pan in air fryer basket and cook. It will be done until golden brown. 7. Repeat the steps with remaining French toast sticks. 8. Serve with maple syrup.

Jalapeño Popper Egg Cups

Prep time: 10 minutes | Cook time: 10 minutes | Serves 2

4 large eggs

¼ cup chopped pickled jalapeños

2 ounces (57 g) full-fat cream cheese

½ cup shredded sharp Cheddar cheese

1. Select Preheat, adjust the temperature to 320°F (160°C), set time to 10 minutes and press Start/Pause. 2. In a medium bowl, beat the eggs, then pour into four silicone muffin cups. 3. In a large microwave-safe bowl, place jalapeños, cream cheese, and Cheddar. Microwave for 30 seconds and stir. Take a spoonful, approximately ¼ of the mixture, and place it in the center of one of the egg cups. Repeat with remaining mixture. 4. Once preheated, place egg cups into the air fryer basket and cook. 5. Serve warm.

Whole Wheat Blueberry Muffins

Prep time: 10 minutes | Cook time: 15 minutes | Serves 6

Olive oil cooking spray

½ cup unsweetened applesauce

¼ cup raw honey

½ cup nonfat plain Greek yogurt

1 teaspoon vanilla extract

1 large egg

1½ cups plus 1 tablespoon whole wheat flour, divided

½ teaspoon baking soda

½ teaspoon baking powder

½ teaspoon salt

½ cup blueberries, fresh or frozen

1. Select Preheat, adjust the temperature to 360°F (182°C), set time to 12 to 15 minutes and press Start/Pause. Lightly coat the inside of six silicone muffin cups or a six-cup muffin tin with olive oil cooking spray. 2. In a large bowl, combine the applesauce, honey, yogurt, vanilla, and egg and mix until smooth. 3. Sift in 1½ cups of the flour, the baking soda, baking powder, and salt into the wet mixture, then stir until just combined. 4. In a small bowl, toss the blueberries with the remaining 1 tablespoon flour, then fold the mixture into the muffin batter. 5. Once preheated, divide the mixture evenly among the prepared muffin cups and place into the basket of the air fryer. The muffins will be done until golden brown on top and a toothpick inserted into the middle of one of the muffins comes out clean. 6. Allow to cool for 5 minutes before serving.

Two-Cheese Grits

Prep time: 10 minutes | Cook time: 10 to 12 minutes | Serves 4

⅔ cup instant grits

1 teaspoon salt

1 teaspoon freshly ground black pepper

¾ cup milk, whole or 2%

1 large egg, beaten

3 ounces (85 g) cream cheese, at room temperature

1 tablespoon butter, melted

1 cup shredded mild Cheddar cheese

1 to 2 tablespoons oil

1. Select Preheat, adjust the temperature to 400°F (204°C), set time to 5 minutes and press Start/Pause. Spritz a baking pan with oil. 2. In a large bowl, combine the grits, salt, and pepper. Stir in the milk, egg, cream cheese, and butter until blended. Stir in the Cheddar cheese. 3. Pour the grits mixture into the prepared pan and place it in the air fryer basket. 4. Once preheated, place the pan into the air fryer basket and cook. Stir the mixture and cook for 5 minutes more for soupy grits or 7 minutes more for firmer grits.

Soufflé

Prep time: 10 minutes | Cook time: 22 minutes | Serves 4

⅓ cup butter, melted
¼ cup flour
1 cup milk
1 ounce (28 g) sugar
4 egg yolks

1 teaspoon vanilla extract
6 egg whites
1 teaspoon cream of tartar
Cooking spray

1. In a bowl, mix the butter and flour until a smooth consistency is achieved. 2. Pour the milk into a saucepan over medium-low heat. Add the sugar and allow to dissolve before raising the heat to boil the milk. 3. Pour in the flour and butter mixture and stir rigorously for 7 minutes to eliminate any lumps. Make sure the mixture thickens. Take off the heat and allow to cool for 15 minutes. 4. Select Preheat, adjust the temperature to 320°F (160°C), set time to 15 minutes and press Start/Pause. 5. Spritz 6 soufflé dishes with cooking spray. 6. Put the egg yolks and vanilla extract in a separate bowl and beat them together with a fork. Pour in the milk and combine well to incorporate everything. 7. In a smaller bowl mix the egg whites and cream of tartar with a fork. Fold into the egg yolks-milk mixture before adding in the flour mixture. Transfer equal amounts to the 6 soufflé dishes. 8. Once preheated, put the dishes in the air fryer and cook. 9. Serve warm.

Buffalo Egg Cups

Prep time: 10 minutes | Cook time: 15 minutes | Serves 2

4 large eggs
2 ounces (57 g) full-fat cream cheese

2 tablespoons buffalo sauce
½ cup shredded sharp Cheddar cheese

1. Select Preheat, adjust the temperature to 320°F (160°C), set time to 15 minutes and press Start/Pause. 2. Crack eggs into two ramekins. 3. In a small microwave-safe bowl, mix cream cheese, buffalo sauce, and Cheddar. Microwave for 20 seconds and then stir. Place a spoonful into each ramekin on top of the eggs. 4. Once preheated, place ramekins into the air fryer basket and cook. Serve warm.

Egg Tarts

Prep time: 10 minutes | Cook time: 17 to 20 minutes | Makes 2 tarts

⅓ sheet frozen puff pastry, thawed
Cooking oil spray
½ cup shredded Cheddar cheese

2 eggs
¼ teaspoon salt, divided
1 teaspoon minced fresh parsley (optional)

1. Select Preheat, adjust the temperature to 390°F (199°C), set time to 17 to 20 minutes and press Start/Pause. 2. Lay the puff pastry sheet on a piece of parchment paper and cut it in half. 3. Once preheated, spray the parchment paper with cooking oil. Transfer the 2 squares of pastry to the basket and cook, keeping them on the parchment paper. 4. After 10 minutes, use a metal spoon to press down the center of each pastry square to make a well. Divide the cheese equally between the baked pastries. Carefully crack an egg on top of the cheese, and sprinkle each with the salt. Resume cooking for 7 to 10 minutes. 5. When the cooking is complete, the eggs will be cooked through. Sprinkle each with parsley (if using) and serve.

Tomato and Cheddar Rolls

Prep time: 30 minutes | Cook time: 25 minutes | Makes 12 rolls

4 Roma tomatoes
½ clove garlic, minced
1 tablespoon olive oil
¼ teaspoon dried thyme
Salt and freshly ground black pepper, to taste
4 cups all-purpose flour

1 teaspoon active dry yeast
2 teaspoons sugar
2 teaspoons salt
1 tablespoon olive oil
1 cup grated Cheddar cheese, plus more for sprinkling at the end
1½ cups water

1. Select Preheat, adjust the temperature to 390°F (199°C), set time to 10 minutes and press Start/Pause. 2. Cut the Roma tomatoes in half, remove the seeds with your fingers and transfer to a bowl. Add the garlic, olive oil, dried thyme, salt and freshly ground black pepper and toss well. 3. Once preheated, place the tomatoes, cut side up in the air fryer basket and cook. The tomatoes should just start to brown. Shake the basket to redistribute the tomatoes, and cook for another 5 to 10 minutes at 330°F (166°C) until the tomatoes are no longer juicy. Let the tomatoes cool and then rough chop them. 4. Combine the flour, yeast, sugar and salt in the bowl of a stand mixer. Add the olive oil, chopped roasted tomatoes and Cheddar cheese to the flour mixture and start to mix using the dough hook attachment. As you're mixing, add 1¼ cups of the water, mixing until the dough comes together. Continue to knead the dough with the dough hook for another 10 minutes, adding enough water to the dough to get it to the right consistency. 5. Transfer the dough to an oiled bowl, cover with a clean kitchen towel and let it rest and rise until it has doubled in volume, about 1 to 2 hours. Then, divide the dough into 12 equal portions. Roll each portion of dough into a ball. Lightly coat each dough ball with oil and let the dough balls rest and rise a second time, covered lightly with plastic wrap for 45 minutes. (Alternately, you can place the rolls in the refrigerator overnight and take them out 2 hours before you bake them.) 6. Select Preheat, adjust the temperature to 360°F (182°C), set time to 10 minutes and press Start/Pause. 7. Once preheated, spray the dough balls and the air fryer basket with a little olive oil. Place three rolls at a time in the basket and cook. Add a little grated Cheddar cheese on top of the rolls for the last 2 minutes of air frying for an attractive finish.

Homemade Cherry Breakfast Tarts

Prep time: 15 minutes | Cook time: 20 minutes | Serves 6

Tarts:
2 refrigerated piecrusts
⅓ cup cherry preserves
Frosting:
½ cup vanilla yogurt
1 ounce (28 g) cream cheese

1 teaspoon cornstarch
Cooking oil

1 teaspoon stevia
Rainbow sprinkles

1. Select Preheat, adjust the temperature to 375°F (191°C), set time to 10 minutes and press Start/Pause. **Make the Tarts:** 2. Place the piecrusts on a flat surface. Using a knife or pizza cutter, cut each piecrust into 3 rectangles, for 6 total. (I discard the unused dough left from slicing the edges.) 3. In a small bowl, combine the preserves and cornstarch. Mix well. 4. Scoop 1 tablespoon of the preserves mixture onto the top half of each piece of piecrust. 5. Fold the bottom of each piece up to close the tart. Using the back of a fork, press along the edges of each tart to seal. 6. Spray the breakfast tarts with cooking oil and place them in the air fryer. I do not recommend stacking the breakfast tarts. They will stick together if stacked. You may need to prepare them in two batches. Allow the breakfast tarts to cool fully before cooking. 7. Once preheated, place the tarts into air fryer basket and cook. 8. If necessary, repeat the steps for the remaining breakfast tarts. **Make the Frosting:** 9. In a small bowl, combine the yogurt, cream cheese, and stevia. Mix well. 10. Spread the breakfast tarts with frosting and top with sprinkles, and serve.

Double-Dipped Mini Cinnamon Biscuits

2 cups blanched almond flour

½ cup Swerve confectioners'-style sweetener or equivalent amount of liquid or powdered sweetener

1 teaspoon baking powder

½ teaspoon fine sea salt

¼ cup plus 2 tablespoons (¾ stick) very cold unsalted butter

¼ cup unsweetened, unflavored almond milk

1 large egg

1 teaspoon vanilla extract

3 teaspoons ground cinnamon

Glaze:

½ cup Swerve confectioners'-style sweetener or equivalent amount of powdered sweetener

¼ cup heavy cream or unsweetened, unflavored almond milk

1. Select Preheat, adjust the temperature to 350°F (177°C), set time to 10 to 13 minutes and press Start/Pause. Line a pie pan that fits into your air fryer with parchment paper. 2. In a medium-sized bowl, mix together the almond flour, sweetener (if powdered; do not add liquid sweetener), baking powder, and salt. Cut the butter into ½-inch squares, then use a hand mixer to work the butter into the dry ingredients. When you are done, the mixture should still have chunks of butter. 3. In a small bowl, whisk together the almond milk, egg, and vanilla extract (if using liquid sweetener, add it as well) until blended. Using a fork, stir the wet ingredients into the dry ingredients until large clumps form. Add the cinnamon and use your hands to swirl it into the dough. 4. Form the dough into sixteen 1-inch balls and put them on the prepared pan, spacing them about ½ inch apart. (If you're using a smaller air fryer, work in batches if necessary.) 5. Once preheated, place the pan into the air fryer and cook. When finished, remove from the air fryer and let cool on the pan for at least 5 minutes. **Make the Glaze:** 6. While the biscuits bake, place the powdered sweetener in a small bowl and slowly stir in the heavy cream with a fork. 7. When the biscuits have cooled somewhat, dip the tops into the glaze, allow it to dry a bit, and then dip again for a thick glaze. 8. Serve warm or at room temperature. Store unglazed biscuits in an airtight container in the refrigerator for up to 3 days or in the freezer for up to a month. Reheat in a preheated 350°F (177°C) air fryer for 5 minutes, or until warmed through, and dip in the glaze as instructed above.

Chapter 2   Poultry

Mediterranean Stuffed Chicken Breasts

Prep time: 5 minutes | Cook time: 20 to 25 minutes | Serves 4

4 small boneless, skinless chicken breast halves (about 1½ pounds / 680 g)

Salt and freshly ground black pepper, to taste

4 ounces (113 g) goat cheese

6 pitted Kalamata olives, coarsely chopped

Zest of ½ lemon

1 teaspoon minced fresh rosemary or ½ teaspoon ground dried rosemary

½ cup almond meal

¼ cup balsamic vinegar

6 tablespoons unsalted butter

1. Select Preheat, adjust the temperature to 360ºF (182ºC), set time to 20 to 25 minutes and press Start/Pause. 2. With a boning knife, cut a wide pocket into the thickest part of each chicken breast half, taking care not to cut all the way through. Season the chicken evenly on both sides with salt and freshly ground black pepper. 3. In a small bowl, mix the cheese, olives, lemon zest, and rosemary. Stuff the pockets with the cheese mixture and secure with toothpicks. 4. Place the almond meal in a shallow bowl and dredge the chicken, shaking off the excess. Coat lightly with olive oil spray. 5. Once preheated, arrange the chicken breasts in the air fryer basket and cook, working in batches if necessary. Pausing halfway through the cooking time to flip the chicken. It will be done until a thermometer inserted into the thickest part registers 165ºF (74ºC). 6. While the chicken is baking, prepare the sauce. In a small pan over medium heat, simmer the balsamic vinegar until thick and syrupy, about 5 minutes. Set aside until the chicken is done. When ready to serve, warm the sauce over medium heat and whisk in the butter, 1 tablespoon at a time, until melted and smooth. Season to taste with salt and pepper. 7. Serve the chicken breasts with the sauce drizzled on top.

Chicken Breasts with Asparagus, Beans, and Arugula

Prep time: 20 minutes | Cook time: 25 minutes | Serves 2

1 cup canned cannellini beans, rinsed

1½ tablespoons red wine vinegar

1 garlic clove, minced

2 tablespoons extra-virgin olive oil, divided

Salt and ground black pepper, to taste

½ red onion, sliced thinly

8 ounces (227 g) asparagus, trimmed and cut into 1-inch

lengths

2 (8-ounce / 227-g) boneless, skinless chicken breasts, trimmed

¼ teaspoon paprika

½ teaspoon ground coriander

2 ounces (57 g) baby arugula, rinsed and drained

1. Select Preheat, adjust the temperature to 400ºF (204ºC), set time to 2 minutes and press Start/Pause. 2. Warm the beans in microwave for 1 minutes and combine with red wine vinegar, garlic, 1 tablespoon of olive oil, ¼ teaspoon of salt, and ¼ teaspoon of ground black pepper in a bowl. Stir to mix well. 3. Combine the onion with ⅛ teaspoon of salt, ⅛ teaspoon of ground black pepper, and 2 teaspoons of olive oil in a separate bowl. Toss to coat well. 4. Once preheated, place the onion in the air fryer basket and cook, then add the asparagus and air fry for 8 more minutes or until the asparagus is tender. Shake the basket halfway through. Transfer the onion and asparagus to the bowl with beans. Set aside. 5. Toss the chicken breasts with remaining ingredients, except for the baby arugula, in a large bowl. 6. Put the chicken breasts in the air fryer basket and cook for 14 minutes or until the internal temperature of the chicken reaches at least 165ºF (74ºC). Flip the breasts halfway through. 7. Remove the chicken from the air fryer and serve on an aluminum foil with asparagus, beans, onion, and arugula. Sprinkle with salt and ground black pepper. Toss to serve.

Spinach and Feta Stuffed Chicken Breasts

Prep time: 10 minutes | Cook time: 27 minutes | Serves 4

1 (10-ounce / 283-g) package frozen spinach, thawed and drained well

1 cup feta cheese, crumbled

½ teaspoon freshly ground black pepper

4 boneless chicken breasts

Salt and freshly ground black pepper, to taste

1 tablespoon olive oil

1. Select Preheat, adjust the temperature to 380°F (193°C), set time to 12 minutes and press Start/Pause. 2. Prepare the filling. Squeeze out as much liquid as possible from the thawed spinach. Rough chop the spinach and transfer it to a mixing bowl with the feta cheese and the freshly ground black pepper. 3. Prepare the chicken breast. Place the chicken breast on a cutting board and press down on the chicken breast with one hand to keep it stabilized. Make an incision about 1-inch long in the fattest side of the breast. Move the knife up and down inside the chicken breast, without poking through either the top or the bottom, or the other side of the breast. The inside pocket should be about 3-inches long, but the opening should only be about 1-inch wide. If this is too difficult, you can make the incision longer, but you will have to be more careful when cooking the chicken breast since this will expose more of the stuffing. 4. Once you have prepared the chicken breasts, use your fingers to stuff the filling into each pocket, spreading the mixture down as far as you can. 5. Once preheated, lightly brush or spray the air fryer basket and the chicken breasts with olive oil. Transfer two of the stuffed chicken breasts to the air fryer basket and cook. Turning the chicken breasts over halfway through the cooking time. 6. Remove the chicken to a resting plate and cook the second two breasts for 12 minutes. Return the first batch of chicken to the air fryer with the second batch and cook for 3 more minutes. When the chicken is cooked, an instant read thermometer should register 165°F (74°C) in the thickest part of the chicken, as well as in the stuffing. 7. Remove the chicken breasts and let them rest on a cutting board for 2 to 3 minutes. Slice the chicken on the bias and serve with the slices fanned out.

Chicken and Broccoli Casserole

Prep time: 5 minutes | Cook time: 20 to 25 minutes | Serves 4

½ pound (227 g) broccoli, chopped into florets

2 cups shredded cooked chicken

4 ounces (113 g) cream cheese

⅓ cup heavy cream

1½ teaspoons Dijon mustard

½ teaspoon garlic powder

Salt and freshly ground black pepper, to taste

2 tablespoons chopped fresh basil

1 cup shredded Cheddar cheese

1. Select Preheat, adjust the temperature to 390°F (199°C), set time to 20 to 25 minutes and press Start/Pause. Lightly coat a casserole dish that will fit in air fryer, with olive oil and set aside. 2. Place the broccoli in a large glass bowl with 1 tablespoon of water and cover with a microwavable plate. Microwave on high for 2 to 3 minutes until the broccoli is bright green but not mushy. Drain if necessary and add to another large bowl along with the shredded chicken. 3. In the same glass bowl used to microwave the broccoli, combine the cream cheese and cream. Microwave for 30 seconds to 1 minute on high and stir until smooth. Add the mustard and garlic powder and season to taste with salt and freshly ground black pepper. Whisk until the sauce is smooth. 4. Pour the warm sauce over the broccoli and chicken mixture and then add the basil. Using a silicone spatula, gently fold the mixture until thoroughly combined, then top with the cheese. 5. Once preheated, transfer the chicken mixture to the prepared casserole dish and cook. It will be done until warmed through and the cheese has browned.

Jalapeño Popper Hasselback Chicken

Prep time: 10 minutes | Cook time: 19 minutes | Serves 2

Oil, for spraying
2 (8-ounce / 227-g) boneless, skinless chicken breasts
2 ounces (57 g) cream cheese, softened

¼ cup bacon bits
¼ cup chopped pickled jalapeños
½ cup shredded Cheddar cheese, divided

1. Select Preheat, adjust the temperature to 350ºF (177ºC), set time to 14 minutes and press Start/Pause. Line the air fryer basket with parchment and spray lightly with oil. 2. Make multiple cuts across the top of each chicken breast, cutting only halfway through. 3. In a medium bowl, mix together the cream cheese, bacon bits, jalapeños, and ¼ cup of Cheddar cheese. Spoon some of the mixture into each cut. 4. Once preheated, place the chicken in the prepared basket and cook. Scatter the remaining ¼ cup of cheese on top of the chicken and cook for another 2 to 5 minutes, or until the cheese is melted and the internal temperature reaches 165ºF (74ºC).

Pecan-Crusted Chicken Tenders

Prep time: 10 minutes | Cook time: 12 minutes | Serves 4

2 tablespoons mayonnaise
1 teaspoon Dijon mustard
1 pound (454 g) boneless, skinless chicken tenders

½ teaspoon salt
¼ teaspoon ground black pepper
½ cup chopped roasted pecans, finely ground

1. Select Preheat, adjust the temperature to 375ºF (191ºC), set time to 12 minutes and press Start/Pause. 2. In a small bowl, whisk mayonnaise and mustard until combined. Brush mixture onto chicken tenders on both sides, then sprinkle tenders with salt and pepper. 3. Place pecans in a medium bowl and press each tender into pecans to coat each side. 4. Once preheated, place tenders into ungreased air fryer basket and cook, working in batches if needed. Turning tenders halfway through cooking. Tenders will be golden brown and have an internal temperature of at least 165ºF (74ºC) when done. Serve warm.

Fried Chicken Breasts

Prep time: 30 minutes | Cook time: 12 to 14 minutes | Serves 4

1 pound (454 g) boneless, skinless chicken breasts
¾ cup dill pickle juice
¾ cup finely ground blanched almond flour
¾ cup finely grated Parmesan cheese

½ teaspoon sea salt
½ teaspoon freshly ground black pepper
2 large eggs
Avocado oil spray

1. Place the chicken breasts in a zip-top bag or between two pieces of plastic wrap. Using a meat mallet or heavy skillet, pound the chicken to a uniform ½-inch thickness. 2. Place the chicken in a large bowl with the pickle juice. Cover and allow to brine in the refrigerator for up to 2 hours. 3. Select Preheat, adjust the temperature to 400ºF (204ºC), set time to 6 to 7 minutes and press Start/Pause. 4. In a shallow dish, combine the almond flour, Parmesan cheese, salt, and pepper. In a separate, shallow bowl, beat the eggs. 5. Drain the chicken and pat it dry with paper towels. Dip in the eggs and then in the flour mixture, making sure to press the coating into the chicken. Spray both sides of the coated breasts with oil. 6. Once preheated, spray the air fryer basket with oil. Put the chicken inside and cook. Carefully flip the breasts with a spatula. Spray the breasts again with oil and continue cooking for 6 to 7 minutes more, until golden and crispy.

Cilantro Chicken Kebabs

Prep time: 30 minutes | Cook time: 10 minutes | Serves 4

Chutney:

½ cup unsweetened shredded coconut

½ cup hot water

2 cups fresh cilantro leaves, roughly chopped

¼ cup fresh mint leaves, roughly chopped

Chicken:

1 pound (454 g) boneless, skinless chicken thighs, cut crosswise into thirds

6 cloves garlic, roughly chopped

1 jalapeño, seeded and roughly chopped

¼ to ¾ cup water, as needed

Juice of 1 lemon

Olive oil spray

Make the Chutney: 1. In a blender or food processor, combine the coconut and hot water; set aside to soak for 5 minutes. 2. To the processor, add the cilantro, mint, garlic, and jalapeño, along with ¼ cup water. Blend at low speed, stopping occasionally to scrape down the sides. Add the lemon juice. With the blender or processor running, add only enough additional water to keep the contents moving. Turn the blender to high once the contents are moving freely and blend until the mixture is puréed. **Make the Chicken:** 3. Place the chicken pieces in a large bowl. Add ¼ cup of the chutney and mix well to coat. Set aside the remaining chutney to use as a dip. Marinate the chicken for 15 minutes at room temperature. 4. Select Preheat, adjust the temperature to 350ºF (177ºC), set time to 10 minutes and press Start/Pause. 5. Once preheated, spray the air fryer basket with olive oil spray, arrange the chicken in the air fryer basket and cook. Use a meat thermometer to ensure that the chicken has reached an internal temperature of 165ºF (74ºC). 6. Serve the chicken with the remaining chutney.

French Garlic Chicken

Prep time: 30 minutes | Cook time: 27 minutes | Serves 4

2 tablespoon extra-virgin olive oil

1 tablespoon Dijon mustard

1 tablespoon apple cider vinegar

3 cloves garlic, minced

2 teaspoons herbes de Provence

½ teaspoon kosher salt

1 teaspoon black pepper

1 pound (454 g) boneless, skinless chicken thighs, halved crosswise

2 tablespoons butter

8 cloves garlic, chopped

¼ cup heavy whipping cream

1. In a small bowl, combine the olive oil, mustard, vinegar, minced garlic, herbes de Provence, salt, and pepper. Use a wire whisk to emulsify the mixture. 2. Pierce the chicken all over with a fork to allow the marinade to penetrate better. Place the chicken in a resealable plastic bag, pour the marinade over, and seal. Massage until the chicken is well coated. Marinate at room temperature for 30 minutes or in the refrigerator for up to 24 hours. 3. When you are ready to cook, select Preheat, adjust the temperature to 400ºF (204ºC), set time to 5 minutes and press Start/Pause. 4. Once preheated, put the butter and chopped garlic in a baking pan and place it in the air fryer basket. It will be done when the butter has melted and the garlic is sizzling. 5. Add the chicken and the marinade to the seasoned butter. Adjust the temperature to 350ºF (177ºC) for 15 minutes. Use a meat thermometer to ensure the chicken has reached an internal temperature of 165ºF (74ºC). Transfer the chicken to a plate and cover lightly with foil to keep warm. 6. Add the cream to the pan, stirring to combine with the garlic, butter, and cooking juices. Place the pan in the air fryer basket and cook. Adjust the temperature to 350ºF (177ºC) for 7 minutes. 7. Pour the thickened sauce over the chicken and serve.

Chicken with Pineapple and Peach

Prep time: 10 minutes | Cook time: 14 to 15 minutes | Serves 4

1 pound (454 g) low-sodium boneless, skinless chicken breasts, cut into 1-inch pieces
1 medium red onion, chopped
1 (8-ounce / 227-g) can pineapple chunks, drained, ¼ cup juice reserved
1 tablespoon peanut oil or safflower oil
1 peach, peeled, pitted, and cubed
1 tablespoon cornstarch
½ teaspoon ground ginger
¼ teaspoon ground allspice
Brown rice, cooked (optional)

1. Select Preheat, adjust the temperature to 380ºF (193ºC), set time to 9 minutes and press Start/Pause. 2. In a medium metal bowl, mix the chicken, red onion, pineapple, and peanut oil. 3. Once preheated, place the bowl into the air fryer basket and cook. When done, remove and stir. 4. Add the peach and return the bowl to the air fryer. Cook for 3 minutes more. Remove and stir again. 5. In a small bowl, whisk the reserved pineapple juice, the cornstarch, ginger, and allspice well. Add to the chicken mixture and stir to combine. 6. Cook for 2 to 3 minutes more, or until the chicken reaches an internal temperature of 165ºF (74ºC) on a meat thermometer and the sauce is slightly thickened. 7. Serve immediately over hot cooked brown rice, if desired.

Chapter 3   Fish and Seafood

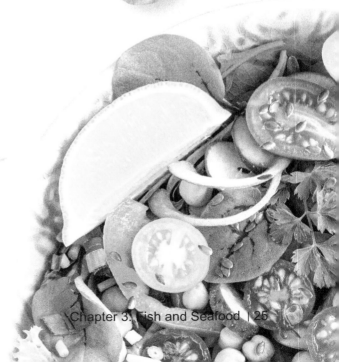

Salmon Spring Rolls

Prep time: 20 minutes | Cook time: 8 to 10 minutes | Serves 4

½ pound (227 g) salmon fillet
1 teaspoon toasted sesame oil
1 onion, sliced
8 rice paper wrappers

1 yellow bell pepper, thinly sliced
1 carrot, shredded
⅓ cup chopped fresh flat-leaf parsley
¼ cup chopped fresh basil

1. Select Preheat, adjust the temperature to 370°F, set time to 8 to 10 minutes and press Start/Pause. 2. Once preheated, put the salmon in the air fryer basket and drizzle with the sesame oil. Add the onion. It will be done when the salmon just flakes if tested with a fork and the onion is tender. 3. Meanwhile, fill a small shallow bowl with warm water. One at a time, dip the rice paper wrappers into the water and place on a work surface. 4. Top each wrapper with one-eighth each of the salmon and onion mixture, yellow bell pepper, carrot, parsley, and basil. Roll up the wrapper, folding in the sides, to enclose the ingredients. 5. If you like, Adjust the temperature to 380°F (193°C), cook for 7 to 9 minutes or until the rolls are crunchy. Cut the rolls in half to serve.

Savory Shrimp

Prep time: 5 minutes | Cook time: 8 to 10 minutes | Serves 4

1 pound (454 g) fresh large shrimp, peeled and deveined
1 tablespoon avocado oil
2 teaspoons minced garlic, divided
½ teaspoon red pepper flakes

Sea salt and freshly ground black pepper, to taste
2 tablespoons unsalted butter, melted
2 tablespoons chopped fresh parsley

1. Select Preheat, adjust the temperature to 350°F (177°C), set time to 6 minutes and press Start/Pause. 2. Place the shrimp in a large bowl and toss with the avocado oil, 1 teaspoon of minced garlic, and red pepper flakes. Season with salt and pepper. 3. Once preheated, place the shrimp into the air fryer basket and cook. Working in batches if necessary. Flip the shrimp and cook for 2 to 4 minutes more, until the internal temperature of the shrimp reaches 120°F (49°C). (The time it takes to cook will depend on the size of the shrimp.) 4. While the shrimp are cooking, melt the butter in a small saucepan over medium heat and stir in the remaining 1 teaspoon of garlic. 5. Transfer the cooked shrimp to a large bowl, add the garlic butter, and toss well. Top with the parsley and serve warm.

Tuna-Stuffed Tomatoes

Prep time: 5 minutes | Cook time: 5 minutes | Serves 2

2 medium beefsteak tomatoes, tops removed, seeded, membranes removed
2 (2.6-ounce / 74-g) pouches tuna packed in water, drained
1 medium stalk celery, trimmed and chopped

2 tablespoons mayonnaise
¼ teaspoon salt
¼ teaspoon ground black pepper
2 teaspoons coconut oil
¼ cup shredded mild Cheddar cheese

1. Select Preheat, adjust the temperature to 320°F (160°C), set time to 5 minutes and press Start/Pause. 2. Scoop pulp out of each tomato, leaving ½-inch shell. 3. In a medium bowl, mix tuna, celery, mayonnaise, salt, and pepper. Drizzle with coconut oil. Spoon ½ mixture into each tomato and top each with 2 tablespoons Cheddar. 4. Once preheated, place tomatoes into ungreased air fryer basket and cook. Cheese will be melted when done. Serve warm.

Coconut Shrimp

Prep time: 5 minutes | Cook time: 6 minutes | Serves 2

8 ounces (227 g) medium shelled and deveined shrimp
2 tablespoons salted butter, melted

½ teaspoon Old Bay seasoning
¼ cup unsweetened shredded coconut

1. Select Preheat, adjust the temperature to 400°F (204°C), set time to 6 minutes and press Start/Pause. 2. In a large bowl, toss the shrimp in butter and Old Bay seasoning. 2. Place shredded coconut in bowl and coat each piece of shrimp in the coconut. Place the coated shrimp into the air fryer basket and cook. 3. Gently turn the shrimp halfway through the cooking time. Serve immediately.

Creamy Haddock

Prep time: 10 minutes | Cook time: 8 minutes | Serves 4

1 pound (454 g) haddock fillet
1 teaspoon cayenne pepper
1 teaspoon salt

1 teaspoon coconut oil
½ cup heavy cream

1. Select Preheat, adjust the temperature to 375°F (191°C), set time to 8 minutes and press Start/Pause. 2. Grease a baking pan with coconut oil. 3. Then put haddock fillet inside and sprinkle it with cayenne pepper, salt, and heavy cream. 4. Once preheated, put the baking pan in the air fryer basket and cook.

Swordfish Skewers with Caponata

Prep time: 15 minutes | Cook time: 20 minutes | Serves 2

1 (10-ounce / 283-g) small Italian eggplant, cut into 1-inch pieces
6 ounces (170 g) cherry tomatoes
3 scallions, cut into 2 inches long
2 tablespoons extra-virgin olive oil, divided
Salt and pepper, to taste
12 ounces (340 g) skinless swordfish steaks, 1¼ inches thick, cut into 1-inch pieces

2 teaspoons honey, divided
2 teaspoons ground coriander, divided
1 teaspoon grated lemon zest, divided
1 teaspoon juice
4 (6-inch) wooden skewers
1 garlic clove, minced
½ teaspoon ground cumin
1 tablespoon chopped fresh basil

1. Select Preheat, adjust the temperature to 400°F (204°C), set time to 14 minutes and press Start/Pause. 2. Toss eggplant, tomatoes, and scallions with 1 tablespoon oil, ¼ teaspoon salt, and ⅛ teaspoon pepper in bowl; transfer to air fryer basket and cook, once preheated. It will be done until eggplant is softened and browned and tomatoes have begun to burst. 3. Tossing halfway through cooking. Transfer vegetables to cutting board and set aside to cool slightly. 4. Pat swordfish dry with paper towels. Combine 1 teaspoon oil, 1 teaspoon honey, 1 teaspoon coriander, ½ teaspoon lemon zest, ⅛ teaspoon salt, and pinch pepper in a clean bowl. Add swordfish and toss to coat. Thread swordfish onto skewers, leaving about ¼ inch between each piece (3 or 4 pieces per skewer). 5. Arrange skewers in air fryer basket, spaced evenly apart. (Skewers may overlap slightly.) Return basket to air fryer and cook for 6 to 8 minutes or until swordfish is browned and registers 140°F (60°C). Flipping and rotating skewers halfway through cooking. 6. Meanwhile, combine remaining 2 teaspoons oil, remaining 1 teaspoon honey, remaining 1 teaspoon coriander, remaining ½ teaspoon lemon zest, lemon juice, garlic, cumin, ¼ teaspoon salt, and ⅛ teaspoon pepper in large bowl. Microwave, stirring once, until fragrant, about 30 seconds. 7. Coarsely chop the cooked vegetables, transfer to bowl with dressing, along with any accumulated juices, and gently toss to combine. 8. Stir in basil and season with salt and pepper to taste. Serve skewers with caponata.

Salmon Patties

12 ounces (340 g) pouched pink salmon
3 tablespoons mayonnaise
⅓ cup blanched finely ground almond flour

½ teaspoon Cajun seasoning
1 medium avocado, peeled, pitted, and sliced

1. Select Preheat, adjust the temperature to 400ºF (204ºC), set time to 8 minutes and press Start/Pause. 2. In a medium bowl, mix salmon, mayonnaise, flour, and Cajun seasoning. Form mixture into four patties. 3. Once preheated, place patties into ungreased air fryer basket and cook. Turning patties halfway through cooking. Patties will be done when firm and golden brown. 4. Transfer patties to four medium plates and serve warm with avocado slices.

Tilapia Almondine

½ cup almond flour or fine dried bread crumbs
2 tablespoons salted butter or ghee, melted
1 teaspoon black pepper
½ teaspoon kosher salt

¼ cup mayonnaise
2 tilapia fillets
½ cup thinly sliced almonds
Vegetable oil spray

1. Select Preheat, adjust the temperature to 325ºF (163ºC), set time to 10 minutes and press Start/Pause. 2. In a small bowl, mix together the almond flour, butter, pepper and salt. 3. Spread the mayonnaise on both sides of each fish fillet. Dredge the fillets in the almond flour mixture. Spread the sliced almonds on one side of each fillet, pressing lightly to adhere. 4. Once preheated, spray the air fryer basket with vegetable oil spray. Place the fish fillets in the basket and cook.. It will be done when fish flakes easily with a fork.

Classic Fish Sticks with Tartar Sauce

1½ pounds (680 g) cod fillets, cut into 1-inch strips
1 teaspoon salt
½ teaspoon freshly ground black pepper
2 eggs
¾ cup almond flour
¼ cup grated Parmesan cheese
Tartar Sauce:

½ cup sour cream
½ cup mayonnaise
3 tablespoons chopped dill pickle
2 tablespoons capers, drained and chopped
½ teaspoon dried dill
1 tablespoon dill pickle liquid (optional)

1. Select Preheat, adjust the temperature to 400ºF (204ºC), set time to 12 to 15 minutes and press Start/Pause. 2. Season the cod with the salt and black pepper; set aside. 3. In a shallow bowl, lightly beat the eggs. In a second shallow bowl, combine the almond flour and Parmesan cheese. Stir until thoroughly combined. 4. Working with a few pieces at a time, dip the fish into the egg mixture followed by the flour mixture. Press lightly to ensure an even coating. 5. Working in batches if necessary, place the fish into the air fryer basket and spray lightly with olive oil once preheated. Pausing halfway through the cooking time to turn the fish. It will be done until the fish flakes easily with a fork. Let sit in the basket for a few minutes before serving with the tartar sauce. **Make the Tartar Sauce:** 6. In a small bowl, combine the sour cream, mayonnaise, pickle, capers, and dill. If you prefer a thinner sauce, stir in the pickle liquid.

Salmon Burgers

Lemon-Caper Rémoulade:

½ cup mayonnaise

2 tablespoons minced drained capers

2 tablespoons chopped fresh parsley

2 teaspoons fresh lemon juice

Salmon Patties:

1 pound (454 g) wild salmon fillet, skinned and pin bones removed

6 tablespoons panko bread crumbs

¼ cup minced red onion plus ¼ cup slivered for serving

1 garlic clove, minced

1 large egg, lightly beaten

1 tablespoon Dijon mustard

1 teaspoon fresh lemon juice

1 tablespoon chopped fresh parsley

½ teaspoon kosher salt

For Serving:

5 whole wheat potato buns or gluten-free buns

10 butter lettuce leaves

Make the Lemon-Caper Rémoulade: 1. In a small bowl, combine the mayonnaise, capers, parsley, and lemon juice and mix well. **Make the Salmon Patties:** 2. Cut off a 4-ounce (113-g) piece of the salmon and transfer to a food processor. Pulse until it becomes pasty. With a sharp knife, chop the remaining salmon into small cubes. 3. In a medium bowl, combine the chopped and processed salmon with the panko, minced red onion, garlic, egg, mustard, lemon juice, parsley, and salt. Toss gently to combine. Form the mixture into 5 patties about ¾ inch thick. Refrigerate for at least 30 minutes. 4. Select Preheat, adjust the temperature to 400ºF (204ºC), set time to 12 minutes and press Start/Pause. 5. Working in batches, place the patties in the air fryer basket and cook, once preheated. Gently flipping halfway, until golden and cooked through. 6. To serve, transfer each patty to a bun. Top each with 2 lettuce leaves, 2 tablespoons of the rémoulade, and the slivered red onions.

Golden Beer-Battered Cod

2 eggs

1 cup malty beer

1 cup all-purpose flour

½ cup cornstarch

1 teaspoon garlic powder

Salt and pepper, to taste

4 (4-ounce / 113-g) cod fillets

Cooking spray

1. Select Preheat, adjust the temperature to 400ºF (204ºC), set time to 15 minutes and press Start/Pause. 2. In a shallow bowl, beat together the eggs with the beer. In another shallow bowl, thoroughly combine the flour and cornstarch. Sprinkle with the garlic powder, salt, and pepper. 3. Dredge each cod fillet in the flour mixture, then in the egg mixture. Dip each piece of fish in the flour mixture a second time. 4. Once preheated, spritz the air fryer basket with cooking spray. Arrange the cod fillets in the basket and cook. Flip the fillets halfway through the cooking time. The cod will be done when reaches an internal temperature of at least 145ºF (63ºC) on a meat thermometer and the outside is crispy. 6. Let the fish cool for 5 minutes and serve.

Firecracker Shrimp

Prep time: 10 minutes | Cook time: 7 minutes | Serves 4

1 pound (454 g) medium shelled and deveined shrimp
2 tablespoons salted butter, melted
½ teaspoon Old Bay seasoning
¼ teaspoon garlic powder

2 tablespoons sriracha
¼ teaspoon powdered erythritol
¼ cup full-fat mayonnaise
⅛ teaspoon ground black pepper

1. Select Preheat, adjust the temperature to 400ºF (204ºC), set time to 7 minutes and press Start/Pause. 2. In a large bowl, toss shrimp in butter, Old Bay seasoning, and garlic powder. Once preheated, place shrimp into the air fryer basket and cook. 3. Flip the shrimp halfway through the cooking time. Shrimp will be bright pink when fully cooked. 4. In another large bowl, mix sriracha, powdered erythritol, mayonnaise, and pepper. Toss shrimp in the spicy mixture and serve immediately.

Pecan-Crusted Catfish

Prep time: 5 minutes | Cook time: 12 minutes | Serves 4

½ cup pecan meal
1 teaspoon fine sea salt
¼ teaspoon ground black pepper
4 (4-ounce / 113-g) catfish fillets

For Garnish (Optional):
Fresh oregano
Pecan halves

1. Spray the air fryer basket with avocado oil. Select Preheat, adjust the temperature to 375ºF (191ºC), set time to 12 minutes and press Start/Pause. 2. In a large bowl, mix the pecan meal, salt, and pepper. One at a time, dredge the catfish fillets in the mixture, coating them well. Use your hands to press the pecan meal into the fillets. 3. Once preheated, spray the fish with avocado oil and place them in the air fryer basket and cook. The coated catfish will be done until it flakes easily and is no longer translucent in the center, flipping halfway through. 4. Garnish with oregano sprigs and pecan halves, if desired. 5. Store leftovers in an airtight container in the fridge for up to 3 days. Reheat in a preheated 350ºF (177ºC) air fryer for 4 minutes, or until heated through.

Tuna Melt

Prep time: 3 minutes | Cook time: 10 minutes | Serves 1

Oil, for spraying
½ (5-ounce / 142-g) can tuna, drained
1 tablespoon mayonnaise
¼ teaspoon granulated garlic, plus more for garnish

2 teaspoons unsalted butter
2 slices sandwich bread
2 slices Cheddar cheese

1. Select Preheat, adjust the temperature to400ºF (204ºC), set time to 5 minutes and press Start/Pause. 2. Line the air fryer basket with parchment and spray lightly with oil. 3. In a medium bowl, mix together the tuna, mayonnaise, and garlic. 4. Spread 1 teaspoon of butter on each slice of bread and top with a slice of cheese, the tuna mixture, another slice of cheese, and the other slice of bread, butter-side up. 5. Once preheated, place one slice butter-side down in the prepared basket and cook. After 5 minutes, flip, and cook for another 5 minutes, until browned and crispy. 6. Sprinkle with additional garlic before cutting in half and serving.

Tuna Avocado Bites

1 (10-ounce / 283-g) can tuna, drained
¼ cup full-fat mayonnaise
1 stalk celery, chopped

1 medium avocado, peeled, pitted, and mashed
½ cup blanched finely ground almond flour, divided
2 teaspoons coconut oil

1. Select Preheat, adjust the temperature to 400°F (204°C), set time to 7 minutes and press Start/Pause. 2. In a large bowl, mix tuna, mayonnaise, celery, and mashed avocado. Form the mixture into balls. 3. Once preheated, roll balls in almond flour and spritz with coconut oil. Place balls into the air fryer basket and cook. 4. Gently turn tuna bites after 5 minutes. Serve warm.

Cajun and Lemon Pepper Cod

1 tablespoon Cajun seasoning
1 teaspoon salt
½ teaspoon lemon pepper
½ teaspoon freshly ground black pepper
2 (8-ounce / 227-g) cod fillets, cut to fit into the air fryer

basket
Cooking spray
2 tablespoons unsalted butter, melted
1 lemon, cut into 4 wedges

1. Select Preheat, adjust the temperature to 360°F (182°C), set time to 12 minutes and press Start/Pause. Spritz the air fryer basket with cooking spray. 2. Thoroughly combine the Cajun seasoning, salt, lemon pepper, and black pepper in a small bowl. Rub this mixture all over the cod fillets until completely coated. 3. Once preheated, put the fillets in the air fryer basket and brush the melted butter over both sides of each fillet. Flipping the fillets halfway through. It will be done until the fish flakes easily with a fork. 4. Remove the fillets from the basket and serve with fresh lemon wedges.

Asian Swordfish

4 (4-ounce / 113-g) swordfish steaks
½ teaspoon toasted sesame oil
1 jalapeño pepper, finely minced
2 garlic cloves, grated

1 tablespoon grated fresh ginger
½ teaspoon Chinese five-spice powder
⅛ teaspoon freshly ground black pepper
2 tablespoons freshly squeezed lemon juice

1. Select Preheat, adjust the temperature to 380°F (193°C), set time to 6 to 11 minutes and press Start/Pause. 2. Place the swordfish steaks on a work surface and drizzle with the sesame oil. 3. In a small bowl, mix the jalapeño, garlic, ginger, five-spice powder, pepper, and lemon juice. Rub this mixture into the fish and let it stand for 10 minutes. 4. Once preheated, place swordfish in the air fryer basket. The swordfish will be done when reaches an internal temperature of at least 140°F (60°C) on a meat thermometer. Serve immediately.

Salmon with Cauliflower

Prep time: 10 minutes | Cook time: 25 minutes | Serves 4

1 pound (454 g) salmon fillet, diced
1 cup cauliflower, shredded
1 tablespoon dried cilantro

1 tablespoon coconut oil, melted
1 teaspoon ground turmeric
¼ cup coconut cream

1. Select Preheat, adjust the temperature to 350ºF (177ºC), set time to 25 minutes and press Start/Pause. 2. In a baking pan, mix the salmon with cauliflower, dried cilantro, ground turmeric, coconut cream, and coconut oil. 3. Once preheated, place the baking pan into the air fryer basket. Stir the meal every 5 minutes to avoid the burning.

Crab-Stuffed Avocado Boats

Prep time: 5 minutes | Cook time: 7 minutes | Serves 4

2 medium avocados, halved and pitted
8 ounces (227 g) cooked crab meat
¼ teaspoon Old Bay seasoning

2 tablespoons peeled and diced yellow onion
2 tablespoons mayonnaise

1. Select Preheat, adjust the temperature to 350ºF (177ºC), set time to 7 minutes and press Start/Pause. 2. Scoop out avocado flesh in each avocado half, leaving ½ inch around edges to form a shell. Chop scooped-out avocado. 3. In a medium bowl, combine crab meat, Old Bay seasoning, onion, mayonnaise, and chopped avocado. Place ¼ mixture into each avocado shell. 4. Once preheated, place avocado boats into ungreased air fryer basket and cook. Avocado will be browned on the top and mixture will be bubbling when done. Serve warm.

Paprika Crab Burgers

Prep time: 30 minutes | Cook time: 14 minutes | Serves 3

2 eggs, beaten
1 shallot, chopped
2 garlic cloves, crushed
1 tablespoon olive oil
1 teaspoon yellow mustard
1 teaspoon fresh cilantro, chopped

10 ounces (283 g) crab meat
1 teaspoon smoked paprika
½ teaspoon ground black pepper
Sea salt, to taste
¾ cup Parmesan cheese

1. Select Preheat, adjust the temperature to 360ºF (182ºC), set time to 14 minutes and press Start/Pause. 2. In a mixing bowl, thoroughly combine the eggs, shallot, garlic, olive oil, mustard, cilantro, crab meat, paprika, black pepper, and salt. Mix until well combined. 3. Shape the mixture into 6 patties. Roll the crab patties over grated Parmesan cheese, coating well on all sides. Place in your refrigerator for 2 hours.4. Once preheated, spritz the crab patties with cooking oil on both sides. Place the patties into air fryer basket and cook. Serve on dinner rolls if desired. Bon appétit!

Chapter 4   Beef, Pork, and Lamb

Bulgogi Burgers

Burgers:

1 pound (454 g) 85% lean ground beef

¼ cup chopped scallions

2 tablespoons gochujang (Korean red chile paste)

1 tablespoon dark soy sauce

2 teaspoons minced garlic

2 teaspoons minced fresh ginger

2 teaspoons sugar

1 tablespoon toasted sesame oil

½ teaspoon kosher salt

Gochujang Mayonnaise:

¼ cup mayonnaise

¼ cup chopped scallions

1 tablespoon gochujang (Korean red chile paste)

1 tablespoon toasted sesame oil

2 teaspoons sesame seeds

4 hamburger buns

Make the Burgers: 1. In a large bowl, mix the ground beef, scallions, gochujang, soy sauce, garlic, ginger, sugar, sesame oil, and salt. Marinate at room temperature for 30 minutes, or cover and refrigerate for up to 24 hours. 2. Select Preheat, adjust the temperature to 350°F (177°C), set time to 10 minutes and press Start/Pause. 3. Divide the meat into four portions and form them into round patties. Make a slight depression in the middle of each patty with your thumb to prevent them from puffing up into a dome shape while cooking. 4. Once preheated, place the patties in the air fryer basket and cook. Meanwhile, **Make the Gochujang Mayonnaise:** 5. Stir together the mayonnaise, scallions, gochujang, sesame oil, and sesame seeds. 6. At the end of the cooking time, use a meat thermometer to ensure the burgers have reached an internal temperature of 160°F / 71°C (medium). 7. To serve, place the burgers on the buns and top with the mayonnaise.

Fajita Meatball Lettuce Wraps

1 pound (454 g) ground beef (85% lean)

½ cup salsa, plus more for serving if desired

¼ cup chopped onions

¼ cup diced green or red bell peppers

1 large egg, beaten

1 teaspoon fine sea salt

½ teaspoon chili powder

½ teaspoon ground cumin

1 clove garlic, minced

For Serving (Optional):

8 leaves Boston lettuce

Pico de gallo or salsa

Lime slices

1. Spray the air fryer basket with avocado oil. Select Preheat, adjust the temperature to 350°F (177°C), set time to 10 minutes and press Start/Pause. 2. In a large bowl, mix together all the ingredients until well combined. 3. Shape the meat mixture into eight 1-inch balls. Once preheated, place the meatballs in the air fryer basket, leaving a little space between them. It will be done until cooked through and no longer pink inside and the internal temperature reaches 145°F (63°C). 4. Serve each meatball on a lettuce leaf, topped with pico de gallo or salsa, if desired. Serve with lime slices if desired. 5. Store leftovers in an airtight container in the fridge for 3 days or in the freezer for up to a month. Reheat in a preheated 350°F (177°C) air fryer for 4 minutes, or until heated through.

Swedish Meatloaf

1½ pounds (680 g) ground beef (85% lean)

¼ pound (113 g) ground pork

1 large egg (omit for egg-free)

½ cup minced onions

¼ cup tomato sauce

Sauce:

½ cup (1 stick) unsalted butter

½ cup shredded Swiss or mild Cheddar cheese (about 2 ounces / 57 g)

2 ounces (57 g) cream cheese (¼ cup), softened

2 tablespoons dry mustard

2 cloves garlic, minced

2 teaspoons fine sea salt

1 teaspoon ground black pepper, plus more for garnish

⅓ cup beef broth

⅛ teaspoon ground nutmeg

Halved cherry tomatoes, for serving (optional)

1. Select Preheat, adjust the temperature to 390°F (199°C), set time to 35 minutes and press Start/Pause. 2. In a large bowl, combine the ground beef, ground pork, egg, onions, tomato sauce, dry mustard, garlic, salt, and pepper. Using your hands, mix until well combined. 3. Once preheated, place the meatloaf mixture in a loaf pan and place it in the air fryer and cook. It will be done until cooked through and the internal temperature reaches 145°F (63°C). Check the meatloaf after 25 minutes; if it's getting too brown on the top, cover it loosely with foil to prevent burning. **Make the Sauce:** 4. While the meatloaf cooks, heat the butter in a saucepan over medium-high heat until it sizzles and brown flecks appear, stirring constantly to keep the butter from burning. Turn the heat down to low and whisk in the Swiss cheese, cream cheese, broth, and nutmeg. Simmer for at least 10 minutes. The longer it simmers, the more the flavors open up. 5. When the meatloaf is done, transfer it to a serving tray and pour the sauce over it. Garnish with ground black pepper and serve with cherry tomatoes, if desired. Allow the meatloaf to rest for 10 minutes before slicing so it doesn't crumble apart. 6. Store leftovers in an airtight container in the fridge for 3 days or in the freezer for up to a month. Reheat in a preheated 350°F (177°C) air fryer for 4 minutes, or until heated through.

Garlic-Marinated Flank Steak

½ cup avocado oil

¼ cup coconut aminos

1 shallot, minced

1 tablespoon minced garlic

2 tablespoons chopped fresh oregano, or 2 teaspoons

dried

1½ teaspoons sea salt

1 teaspoon freshly ground black pepper

¼ teaspoon red pepper flakes

2 pounds (907 g) flank steak

1. In a blender, combine the avocado oil, coconut aminos, shallot, garlic, oregano, salt, black pepper, and red pepper flakes. Process until smooth. 2. Place the steak in a zip-top plastic bag or shallow dish with the marinade. Seal the bag or cover the dish and marinate in the refrigerator for at least 2 hours or overnight. 3. Select Preheat, adjust the temperature to 400°F (204°C), set time to 4 to 6 minutes and press Start/Pause. 4. Remove the steak from the bag and discard the marinade.. Once preheated, place the steak in the air fryer basket and cook (if needed, cut into sections and work in batches). 5. Flip the steak, and cook for another 4 minutes or until the internal temperature reaches 120°F (49°C) in the thickest part for medium-rare (or as desired).

Pigs in a Blanket

Prep time: 10 minutes | Cook time: 7 minutes | Serves 2

½ cup shredded Mozzarella cheese
2 tablespoons blanched finely ground almond flour
1 ounce (28 g) full-fat cream cheese

2 (2-ounce / 57-g) beef smoked sausages
½ teaspoon sesame seeds

1. Select Preheat, adjust the temperature to 400°F (204°C), set time to 7 minutes and press Start/Pause. 2. Place Mozzarella, almond flour, and cream cheese in a large microwave-safe bowl. Microwave for 45 seconds and stir until smooth. Roll dough into a ball and cut in half. 3. Press each half out into a 4 × 5-inch rectangle. Roll one sausage up in each dough half and press seams closed. Sprinkle the top with sesame seeds. 3. Once preheated, place each wrapped sausage into the air fryer basket and cook. 4. The outside will be golden when completely cooked. Serve immediately.

Bacon-Wrapped Hot Dogs with Mayo-Ketchup

Prep time: 5 minutes | Cook time: 10 to 12 minutes | Serves 5

10 thin slices of bacon
5 pork hot dogs, halved
Sauce:
¼ cup mayonnaise
4 tablespoons low-carb ketchup

1 teaspoon cayenne pepper

1 teaspoon rice vinegar
1 teaspoon chili powder

1. Select Preheat, adjust the temperature to 390°F (199°C), set time to 10 to 12 minutes and press Start/Pause. 2. Arrange the slices of bacon on a clean work surface. One by one, place the halved hot dog on one end of each slice, season with cayenne pepper and wrap the hot dog with the bacon slices and secure with toothpicks as needed. 3. Once preheated, work in batches, place half the wrapped hot dogs in the air fryer basket and cook. The bacon will be done whenbecomes browned and crispy. **Make the Sauce:** 4. Stir all the ingredients for the sauce in a small bowl. Wrap the bowl in plastic and set in the refrigerator until ready to serve. 5. Transfer the hot dogs to a platter and serve hot with the sauce.

Mustard Herb Pork Tenderloin

Prep time: 5 minutes | Cook time: 20 minutes | Serves 6

¼ cup mayonnaise
2 tablespoons Dijon mustard
½ teaspoon dried thyme
¼ teaspoon dried rosemary

1 (1-pound / 454-g) pork tenderloin
½ teaspoon salt
¼ teaspoon ground black pepper

1. Select Preheat, adjust the temperature to 400°F (204°C), set time to 20 minutes and press Start/Pause. 2. In a small bowl, mix mayonnaise, mustard, thyme, and rosemary. Brush tenderloin with mixture on all sides, then sprinkle with salt and pepper on all sides. 3. Once preheated, place tenderloin into ungreased air fryer basket and cook. Turning tenderloin halfway through cooking. Tenderloin will be golden and have an internal temperature of at least 145°F (63°C) when done. Serve warm.

Short Ribs with Chimichurri

Prep time: 30 minutes | Cook time: 13 minutes | Serves 4

1 pound (454 g) boneless short ribs
1½ teaspoons sea salt, divided
½ teaspoon freshly ground black pepper, divided
½ cup fresh parsley leaves
½ cup fresh cilantro leaves
1 teaspoon minced garlic

1 tablespoon freshly squeezed lemon juice
½ teaspoon ground cumin
¼ teaspoon red pepper flakes
2 tablespoons extra-virgin olive oil
Avocado oil spray

1. Pat the short ribs dry with paper towels. Sprinkle the ribs all over with 1 teaspoon salt and ¼ teaspoon black pepper. Let sit at room temperature for 45 minutes. 2. Meanwhile, place the parsley, cilantro, garlic, lemon juice, cumin, red pepper flakes, the remaining ½ teaspoon salt, and the remaining ¼ teaspoon black pepper in a blender or food processor. With the blender running, slowly drizzle in the olive oil. Blend for about 1 minute, until the mixture is smooth and well combined. 3. Select Preheat, adjust the temperature to 400°F (204°C), set time to 8 minutes and press Start/Pause. Spray both sides of the ribs with oil. 4. Once preheated, place in the basket and cook.. When finished, flip and cook for another 5 minutes, until an instant-read thermometer reads 125°F (52°C) for medium-rare (or to your desired doneness). 5. Allow the meat to rest for 5 to 10 minutes, then slice. Serve warm with the chimichurri sauce.

Cheesy Low-Carb Lasagna

Prep time: 10 minutes | Cook time: 10 minutes | Serves 4

Meat Layer:
Extra-virgin olive oil
1 pound (454 g) 85% lean ground beef
1 cup prepared marinara sauce
¼ cup diced celery
Cheese Layer:
8 ounces (227 g) ricotta cheese
1 cup shredded Mozzarella cheese
½ cup grated Parmesan cheese
2 large eggs

¼ cup diced red onion
½ teaspoon minced garlic
Kosher salt and black pepper, to taste

1 teaspoon dried Italian seasoning, crushed
½ teaspoon each minced garlic, garlic powder, and black pepper

Make the Meat Layer: 1. Select Preheat, adjust the temperature to 375°F (191°C), set time to 10 minutes and press Start/Pause. 2. Grease a cake pan with 1 teaspoon olive oil. 2. In a large bowl, combine the ground beef, marinara, celery, onion, garlic, salt, and pepper. Place the seasoned meat in the pan. 3. Once preheated, place the pan in the air fryer basket and cook. Meanwhile, **Make the Cheese Layer:** 4. In a medium bowl, combine the ricotta, half the Mozzarella, the Parmesan, lightly beaten eggs, Italian seasoning, minced garlic, garlic powder, and pepper. Stir until well blended. 5. At the end of the cooking time, spread the cheese mixture over the meat mixture. Sprinkle with the remaining ½ cup Mozzarella. 6. Adjust the temperature to 375°F (191°C), set time to 10 minutes. It will be done until the cheese is browned and bubbling. 7. At the end of the cooking time, use a meat thermometer to ensure the meat has reached an internal temperature of 160°F (71°C). 7. Drain the fat and liquid from the pan. Let stand for 5 minutes before serving.

Ham Hock Mac and Cheese

Prep time: 20 minutes | Cook time: 25 minutes | Serves 4

2 large eggs, beaten

2 cups cottage cheese, whole milk or 2%

2 cups grated sharp Cheddar cheese, divided

1 cup sour cream

½ teaspoon salt

1 teaspoon freshly ground black pepper

2 cups uncooked elbow macaroni

2 ham hocks (about 11 ounces / 312 g each), meat removed and diced

1 to 2 tablespoons oil

1. Select Preheat, adjust the temperature to 360ºF (182ºC), set time to 12 minutes and press Start/Pause. 2. In a large bowl, stir together the eggs, cottage cheese, 1 cup of the Cheddar cheese, sour cream, salt, and pepper. 3. Stir in the macaroni and the diced meat. 4. Spritz a baking pan with oil. Pour the macaroni mixture into the prepared pan, making sure all noodles are covered with sauce. 5. Once preheated. place the baking pan into the air fryer basket and cook. 6. When finished, stir in the remaining 1 cup of Cheddar cheese, making sure all the noodles are covered with sauce. Cook for 13 minutes more, until the noodles are tender. Let rest for 5 minutes before serving.

Kale and Beef Omelet

Prep time: 15 minutes | Cook time: 16 minutes | Serves 4

½ pound (227 g) leftover beef, coarsely chopped

2 garlic cloves, pressed

1 cup kale, torn into pieces and wilted

1 tomato, chopped

¼ teaspoon sugar

4 eggs, beaten

4 tablespoons heavy cream

½ teaspoon turmeric powder

Salt and ground black pepper, to taste

⅛ teaspoon ground allspice

Cooking spray

1. Select Preheat, adjust the temperature to 360ºF (182ºC) set time to 16 minutes. and press Start/Pause.. Spritz four ramekins with cooking spray. 2. Put equal amounts of each of the ingredients into each ramekin and mix well. 3. Once preheated, place the ramekins into the air fryer basket and cook. Serve immediately.

Bean and Beef Meatball Taco Pizza

Prep time: 10 minutes | Cook time: 7 to 9 minutes per batch | Serves 4

¾ cup refried beans (from a 16-ounce / 454-g can)

½ cup salsa

10 frozen precooked beef meatballs, thawed and sliced

1 jalapeño pepper, sliced

4 whole-wheat pita breads

1 cup shredded pepper Jack cheese

½ cup shredded Colby cheese

Cooking oil spray

⅓ cup sour cream

1. Select Preheat, adjust the temperature to 375ºF (191ºC), set time to 7 minutes and press Start/Pause. Line a baking pan with parchment paper. 2. In a medium bowl, stir together the refried beans, salsa, meatballs, and jalapeño. 3. Top the pitas with the refried bean mixture and sprinkle with the cheeses, and put in the baking pan. 4. Once preheated, spray the pan with cooking oil. Working in batches, place the pan into the basket and cook. 5. After about 7 minutes, check the pizzas. They are done when the cheese is melted and starts to brown. If not ready, resume cooking. 6. When the cooking is complete, top each pizza with a dollop of sour cream and serve warm.

Vietnamese "Shaking" Beef

Prep time: 30 minutes | Cook time: 6 minutes per batch | Serves 4

Meat:

4 garlic cloves, minced

2 teaspoons soy sauce

2 teaspoons sugar

1 teaspoon toasted sesame oil

1 teaspoon kosher salt

¼ teaspoon black pepper

1½ pounds (680 g) flat iron or top sirloin steak, cut into 1-inch cubes

Salad:

2 tablespoons rice vinegar or apple cider vinegar

2 tablespoons vegetable oil

1 garlic clove, minced

2 teaspoons sugar

¼ teaspoon kosher salt

¼ teaspoon black pepper

½ red onion, halved and very thinly sliced

1 head Bibb lettuce, leaves separated and torn into large pieces

½ cup halved grape tomatoes

¼ cup fresh mint leaves

For Serving:

Lime wedges

Coarse salt and freshly cracked black pepper, to taste

Make the Meat: 1. In a small bowl, combine the garlic, soy sauce, sugar, sesame oil, salt, and pepper. Place the meat in a gallon-size resealable plastic bag. Pour the marinade over the meat. Seal and place the bag in a large bowl. Marinate for 30 minutes, or cover and refrigerate for up to 24 hours. 2. Select Preheat, adjust the temperature to 400°F (204°C), set time to 6 minutes and press Start/Pause. 3. Once preheated, place half the meat in the air fryer basket and cook. Shaking the basket to redistribute the meat halfway through the cooking time. Transfer the meat to a plate (it should be medium-rare, still pink in the middle). Cover lightly with aluminum foil. Repeat to cook the remaining meat. Meanwhile, **Make the Salad:** 4. In a large bowl, whisk together the vinegar, vegetable oil, garlic, sugar, salt, and pepper. Add the onion. Stir to combine. Add the lettuce, tomatoes, and mint and toss to combine. Arrange the salad on a serving platter. 5. Arrange the cooked meat over the salad. Drizzle any accumulated juices from the plate over the meat. Serve with lime wedges, coarse salt, and cracked black pepper.

Air Fryer Chicken-Fried Steak

Prep time: 5 minutes | Cook time: 20 minutes | Serves 4

1 pound beef chuck sirloin steak

3 cups low-fat milk, divided

1 teaspoon dried thyme

1 teaspoon dried rosemary

2 medium egg whites

1 cup chickpea crumbs

½ cup coconut flour

1 tablespoon Creole seasoning

1. In a bowl, marinate the steak in 2 cups of milk for 30 to 45 minutes. 2. Select Preheat, adjust the temperature to 390°F (199°C), set time to 10 minutes and press Start/Pause. 3. Remove the steak from milk, shake off the excess liquid, and season with the thyme and rosemary. Discard the milk. 4. In a shallow bowl, beat the egg whites with the remaining 1 cup of milk. 5. In a separate shallow bowl, combine the chickpea crumbs, coconut flour, and seasoning. 6. Dip the steak in the egg white mixture then dredge in the chickpea crumb mixture, coating well. 7. Once preheated, place the steak in the air fryer basket and cook. 8. Open the air fryer, turn the steaks, close, and cook for 10 minutes. Let rest for 5 minutes.

Chorizo and Beef Burger

Prep time: 10 minutes | Cook time: 15 minutes | Serves 4

¾ pound (340 g) 80/20 ground beef
¼ pound (113 g) Mexican-style ground chorizo
¼ cup chopped onion
5 slices pickled jalapeños, chopped

2 teaspoons chili powder
1 teaspoon minced garlic
¼ teaspoon cumin

1. Select Preheat, adjust the temperature to 375°F (191°C), set time to 15 minutes and press Start/Pause. 2. In a large bowl, mix all ingredients. Divide the mixture into four sections and form them into burger patties. 3. Once preheated, place burger patties into the air fryer basket and cook, working in batches if necessary. 4. Flip the patties halfway through the cooking time. Serve warm.

Beef and Pork Sausage Meatloaf

Prep time: 20 minutes | Cook time: 25 minutes | Serves 4

¾ pound (340 g) ground chuck
4 ounces (113 g) ground pork sausage
1 cup shallots, finely chopped
2 eggs, well beaten
3 tablespoons plain milk
1 tablespoon oyster sauce
1 teaspoon porcini mushrooms

½ teaspoon cumin powder
1 teaspoon garlic paste
1 tablespoon fresh parsley
Salt and crushed red pepper flakes, to taste
1 cup crushed saltines
Cooking spray

1. Select Preheat, adjust the temperature to 360°F (182°C), set time to 25 minutes and press Start/Pause. Spritz a baking dish with cooking spray. 2. Mix all the ingredients in a large bowl, combining everything well. 3. Once preheated, transfer to the baking dish, put into air fryer basket and cook. 4. Serve hot.

Parmesan-Crusted Steak

Prep time: 30 minutes | Cook time: 12 minutes | Serves 6

½ cup (1 stick) unsalted butter, at room temperature
1 cup finely grated Parmesan cheese
¼ cup finely ground blanched almond flour

1½ pounds (680 g) New York strip steak
Sea salt and freshly ground black pepper, to taste

1. Place the butter, Parmesan cheese, and almond flour in a food processor. Process until smooth. Transfer to a sheet of parchment paper and form into a log. Wrap tightly in plastic wrap. Freeze for 45 minutes or refrigerate for at least 4 hours. 2. While the butter is chilling, season the steak liberally with salt and pepper. Let the steak rest at room temperature for about 45 minutes. 3. Select Preheat, adjust the temperature to 400°F (204°C), set time to 4 minutes and press Start/Pause. 4. Once preheated, place the steak in your air fryer and cook. Working in batches, if necessary. Flip and cook for 3 minutes more, until the steak is brown on both sides. 5. Remove the steak from the air fryer and arrange an equal amount of the Parmesan butter on top of each steak. Return the steak to the air fryer and continue cooking for another 5 minutes, until an instant-read thermometer reads 120°F (49°C) for medium-rare and the crust is golden brown (or to your desired doneness). 6. Transfer the cooked steak to a plate; let rest for 10 minutes before serving.

Onion Pork Kebabs

Prep time: 22 minutes | Cook time: 18 minutes | Serves 3

2 tablespoons tomato purée
½ fresh serrano, minced
⅓ teaspoon paprika
1 pound (454 g) pork, ground

½ cup green onions, finely chopped
3 cloves garlic, peeled and finely minced
1 teaspoon ground black pepper, or more to taste
1 teaspoon salt, or more to taste

1. Select Preheat, adjust the temperature to 355°F (179°C), set time to 18 minutes and press Start/Pause. 2. Thoroughly combine all ingredients in a mixing dish. Then form your mixture into sausage shapes. 3. Once preheated, place the sausage in the air fryer basket and cook. 4. Mound salad on a serving platter, top with air-fried kebabs and serve warm. Bon appétit!

Jalapeño Popper Pork Chops

Prep time: 15 minutes | Cook time: 6 to 8 minutes | Serves 4

1¾ pounds (794 g) bone-in, center-cut loin pork chops
Sea salt and freshly ground black pepper, to taste
6 ounces (170 g) cream cheese, at room temperature
4 ounces (113 g) sliced bacon, cooked and crumbled

4 ounces (113 g) Cheddar cheese, shredded
1 jalapeño, seeded and diced
1 teaspoon garlic powder

1. Select Preheat, adjust the temperature to 400°F (204°C), set time to 3 minutes and press Start/Pause. 2. Cut a pocket into each pork chop, lengthwise along the side, making sure not to cut it all the way through. Season the outside of the chops with salt and pepper. 3. In a small bowl, combine the cream cheese, bacon, Cheddar cheese, jalapeño, and garlic powder. Divide this mixture among the pork chops, stuffing it into the pocket of each chop. 4. Once preheated, place the pork chops in the air fryer basket and cook, working in batches if necessary. When finished, flip the chops and cook for 3 to 5 minutes more, until an instant-read thermometer reads 145°F (63°C). 5. Allow the chops to rest for 5 minutes, then serve warm.

Spinach and Provolone Steak Rolls

Prep time: 10 minutes | Cook time: 12 minutes | Makes 8 rolls

1 (1-pound / 454-g) flank steak, butterflied
8 (1-ounce / 28-g, ¼-inch-thick) deli slices provolone cheese

1 cup fresh spinach leaves
½ teaspoon salt
¼ teaspoon ground black pepper

1. Select Preheat, adjust the temperature to 400°F (204°C), set time to 12 minutes and press Start/Pause. 2. Place steak on a large plate. Place provolone slices to cover steak, leaving 1-inch at the edges. Lay spinach leaves over cheese. Gently roll steak and tie with kitchen twine or secure with toothpicks. Carefully slice into eight pieces. Sprinkle each with salt and pepper. 3. Once preheated, place rolls into ungreased air fryer basket, cut side up, and cook. Steak rolls will be browned and cheese will be melted when done and have an internal temperature of at least 150°F (66°C) for medium steak and 180°F (82°C) for well-done steak. Serve warm.

Chapter 5   Vegetarian Mains

Fried Root Vegetable Medley with Thyme

Prep time: 10 minutes | Cook time: 22 minutes | Serves 4

2 carrots, sliced
2 potatoes, cut into chunks
1 rutabaga, cut into chunks
1 turnip, cut into chunks
1 beet, cut into chunks
8 shallots, halved

2 tablespoons olive oil
Salt and black pepper, to taste
2 tablespoons tomato pesto
2 tablespoons water
2 tablespoons chopped fresh thyme

1. Select Preheat, adjust the temperature to 400°F (204°C), set time to 12 minutes and press Start/Pause. 2. Toss the carrots, potatoes, rutabaga, turnip, beet, shallots, olive oil, salt, and pepper in a large mixing bowl until the root vegetables are evenly coated. 3. Once preheated, place the root vegetables in the air fryer basket and cook. When done, shake the basket and cook for another 10 minutes until they are cooked to your preferred doneness. 4. Meanwhile, in a small bowl, whisk together the tomato pesto and water until smooth. 5. When ready, remove the root vegetables from the basket to a platter. Drizzle with the tomato pesto mixture and sprinkle with the thyme. Serve immediately.

Russet Potato Gratin

Prep time: 10 minutes | Cook time: 35 minutes | Serves 6

½ cup milk
7 medium russet potatoes, peeled
Salt, to taste
1 teaspoon black pepper

½ cup heavy whipping cream
½ cup grated semi-mature cheese
½ teaspoon nutmeg

1. Select Preheat, adjust the temperature to 390°F (199°C), set time to 25 minutes and press Start/Pause. 2. Cut the potatoes into wafer-thin slices. 3. In a bowl, combine the milk and cream and sprinkle with salt, pepper, and nutmeg. 4. Use the milk mixture to coat the slices of potatoes. Put in a baking dish. Top the potatoes with the rest of the milk mixture. 5. Once preheated, put the baking dish into the air fryer basket and cook. 6. Pour the cheese over the potatoes. 7. Cook for an additional 10 minutes, ensuring the top is nicely browned before serving.

Potato and Broccoli with Tofu Scramble

Prep time: 15 minutes | Cook time: 30 minutes | Serves 3

2½ cups chopped red potato
2 tablespoons olive oil, divided
1 block tofu, chopped finely
2 tablespoons tamari
1 teaspoon turmeric powder

½ teaspoon onion powder
½ teaspoon garlic powder
½ cup chopped onion
4 cups broccoli florets

1. Select Preheat, adjust the temperature to 400°F (204°C)., set time to 15 minutes and press Start/Pause. 2. Toss together the potatoes and 1 tablespoon of the olive oil. Put in a baking dish. 3. Once preheated, place the baking dish into the air fryer basket and cook, shaking once during the cooking time to ensure they fry evenly. 4. Combine the tofu, the remaining 1 tablespoon of the olive oil, turmeric, onion powder, tamari, and garlic powder together, stirring in the onions, followed by the broccoli. 5. Top the potatoes with the tofu mixture and cook for an additional 15 minutes. Serve warm.

Tangy Asparagus and Broccoli

Prep time: 25 minutes | Cook time: 22 minutes | Serves 4

½ pound (227 g) asparagus, cut into 1 ½-inch pieces
½ pound (227 g) broccoli, cut into 1 ½-inch pieces
2 tablespoons olive oil

Salt and white pepper, to taste
½ cup vegetable broth
2 tablespoons apple cider vinegar

1. Select Preheat, adjust the temperature to 380ºF (193ºC), set time to 15 minutes and press Start/Pause. 2. Drizzle the olive oil over the vegetables and sprinkle with salt and white pepper. 3. Once preheated, place the vegetables in the lightly greased air fryer basket and cook, shaking the basket halfway through the cooking time. 4. Add ½ cup of vegetable broth to a saucepan; bring to a rapid boil and add the vinegar. Cook for 5 to 7 minutes or until the sauce has reduced by half. 5. Spoon the sauce over the warm vegetables and serve immediately. Bon appétit!

Sweet Potatoes with Zucchini

Prep time: 20 minutes | Cook time: 20 minutes | Serves 4

2 large-sized sweet potatoes, peeled and quartered
1 medium zucchini, sliced
1 Serrano pepper, deseeded and thinly sliced
1 bell pepper, deseeded and thinly sliced
1 to 2 carrots, cut into matchsticks
¼ cup olive oil
1½ tablespoons maple syrup

½ teaspoon porcini powder
¼ teaspoon mustard powder
½ teaspoon fennel seeds
1 tablespoon garlic powder
½ teaspoon fine sea salt
¼ teaspoon ground black pepper
Tomato ketchup, for serving

1. Select Preheat, adjust the temperature to 350ºF (177ºC), set time to 15 minutes and press Start/Pause. 2. Once preheated, put the sweet potatoes, zucchini, peppers, and the carrot into the air fryer basket, coat with a drizzling of olive oil and cook. 3. In the meantime, prepare the sauce by vigorously combining the other ingredients, except for the tomato ketchup, with a whisk. 4. Lightly grease a baking dish. 5. Transfer the cooked vegetables to the baking dish, pour over the sauce and coat the vegetables well. 6. Increase the temperature to 390ºF (199ºC) and cook the vegetables for an additional 5 minutes. 7. Serve warm with a side of ketchup.

Broccoli Crust Pizza

Prep time: 15 minutes | Cook time: 12 minutes | Serves 4

3 cups riced broccoli, steamed and drained well
1 large egg
½ cup grated vegetarian Parmesan cheese

3 tablespoons low-carb Alfredo sauce
½ cup shredded Mozzarella cheese

1. Select Preheat, adjust the temperature to 370ºF (188ºC), set time to 5 minutes and press Start/Pause. 2. In a large bowl, mix broccoli, egg, and Parmesan. 3. Cut a piece of parchment to fit your air fryer basket. Press out the pizza mixture to fit on the parchment, working in two batches if necessary. Once preheated, place into the air fryer basket and cook. 4. The crust should be firm enough to flip. If not, add 2 additional minutes. Flip crust. 5. Top with Alfredo sauce and Mozzarella. Return to the air fryer basket and cook an additional 7 minutes or until cheese is golden and bubbling. Serve warm.

Crispy Cabbage Steaks

Prep time: 5 minutes | Cook time: 10 minutes | Serves 4

1 small head green cabbage, cored and cut into ½-inch-thick slices

¼ teaspoon salt

¼ teaspoon ground black pepper

2 tablespoons olive oil

1 clove garlic, peeled and finely minced

½ teaspoon dried thyme

½ teaspoon dried parsley

1. Select Preheat, adjust the temperature to 350°F (177°C), set time to 10 minutes and press Start/Pause. 2. Sprinkle each side of cabbage with salt and pepper and drizzle each side of cabbage with olive oil. 3. Once preheated, place into ungreased air fryer basket, sprinkle with remaining ingredients on both sides and cook, working in batches if needed. Turning "steaks" halfway through cooking. Cabbage will be browned at the edges and tender when done. Serve warm.

Mushroom and Pepper Pizza Squares

Prep time: 10 minutes | Cook time: 10 minutes | Serves 10

1 pizza dough, cut into squares

1 cup chopped oyster mushrooms

1 shallot, chopped

¼ red bell pepper, chopped

2 tablespoons parsley

Salt and ground black pepper, to taste

1. Select Preheat, adjust the temperature to 400°F (204°C), set time to 10 minutes and press Start/Pause. 2. In a bowl, combine the oyster mushrooms, shallot, bell pepper and parsley. Sprinkle some salt and pepper as desired. 3. Spread this mixture on top of the pizza squares. Once preheated, put them in the air fryer basket and cook. 4. Serve warm.

Almond-Cauliflower Gnocchi

Prep time: 5 minutes | Cook time: 25 to 30 minutes | Serves 4

5 cups cauliflower florets

⅔ cup almond flour

½ teaspoon salt

¼ cup unsalted butter, melted

¼ cup grated Parmesan cheese

1. In a food processor fitted with a metal blade, pulse the cauliflower until finely chopped. Transfer the cauliflower to a large microwave-safe bowl and cover it with a paper towel. Microwave for 5 minutes. Spread the cauliflower on a towel to cool. 2. When cool enough to handle, draw up the sides of the towel and squeeze tightly over a sink to remove the excess moisture. Return the cauliflower to the food processor and whirl until creamy. Sprinkle in the flour and salt and pulse until a sticky dough comes together. 3. Select Preheat, adjust the temperature to 400°F (204°C), set time to 25 to 30 minutes and press Start/Pause. 4. Transfer the dough to a workspace lightly floured with almond flour. Shape the dough into a ball and divide into 4 equal sections. Roll each section into a rope 1 inch thick. Slice the dough into squares with a sharp knife. 5. Once preheated, place the gnocchi in the air fryer basket spray generously with olive oil and cook, working in batches if necessary. Pausing halfway through the cooking time to turn the gnocchi. It will be done until golden brown and crispy on the edges. 6. Transfer to a large bowl and toss with the melted butter and Parmesan cheese.

Super Vegetable Burger

Prep time: 15 minutes | Cook time: 12 minutes | Serves 8

½ pound (227 g) cauliflower, steamed and diced, rinsed and drained
2 teaspoons coconut oil, melted
2 teaspoons minced garlic
¼ cup desiccated coconut
½ cup oats
3 tablespoons flour

1 tablespoon flaxseeds plus 3 tablespoons water, divided
1 teaspoon mustard powder
2 teaspoons thyme
2 teaspoons parsley
2 teaspoons chives
Salt and ground black pepper, to taste
1 cup bread crumbs

1. Select Preheat, adjust the temperature to 390°F (199°C), set time to 12 minutes and press Start/Pause. 2. Combine the cauliflower with all the ingredients, except for the bread crumbs, incorporating everything well. 3. Using the hands, shape 8 equal-sized amounts of the mixture into burger patties. Coat the patties in bread crumbs. Once preheated, put them in the air fryer basket and cook. 4. Serve hot.

Sweet Pepper Nachos

Prep time: 10 minutes | Cook time: 5 minutes | Serves 2

6 mini sweet peppers, seeded and sliced in half
¾ cup shredded Colby jack cheese
¼ cup sliced pickled jalapeños

½ medium avocado, peeled, pitted, and diced
2 tablespoons sour cream

1. Select Preheat, adjust the temperature to 350°F (177°C), set time to 5 minutes and press Start/Pause. 2. Place peppers into an ungreased round nonstick baking dish. Sprinkle with Colby and top with jalapeños. 3. Once preheated, place dish into air fryer basket and cook. Cheese will be melted and bubbly when done. 4. Remove dish from air fryer and top with avocado. Drizzle with sour cream. Serve warm.

Buffalo Cauliflower Bites with Blue Cheese

Prep time: 10 minutes | Cook time: 8 to 10 minutes | Serves 4

1 large head cauliflower, chopped into florets
1 tablespoon olive oil
Salt and freshly ground black pepper, to taste
¼ cup unsalted butter, melted
¼ cup hot sauce
Garlic Blue Cheese Dip:

½ cup mayonnaise
¼ cup sour cream
2 tablespoons heavy cream
1 tablespoon fresh lemon juice
1 clove garlic, minced
¼ cup crumbled blue cheese
Salt and freshly ground black pepper, to taste

1. Select Preheat, adjust the temperature to 400°F (204°C), set time to 8 to 10 minutes and press Start/Pause. 2. In a large bowl, combine the cauliflower and olive oil. Season to taste with salt and black pepper. Toss until the vegetables are thoroughly coated. 3. Once preheated, working in batches, place half of the cauliflower in the air fryer basket and cook. Pausing halfway through the cooking time to shake the basket. It will be done until the cauliflower is evenly browned. Transfer to a large bowl and repeat with the remaining cauliflower. 4. In a small bowl, whisk together the melted butter and hot sauce. **Make the Dip:** 5. In a small bowl, combine the mayonnaise, sour cream, heavy cream, lemon juice, garlic, and blue cheese. Season to taste with salt and freshly ground black pepper. 6. Just before serving, pour the butter mixture over the cauliflower and toss gently until thoroughly coated. Serve with the dip on the side.

Crispy Eggplant Slices with Parsley

Prep time: 5 minutes | Cook time: 10 to 12 minutes | Serves 4

1 cup flour
4 eggs
Salt, to taste
2 cups bread crumbs
1 teaspoon Italian seasoning

2 eggplants, sliced
2 garlic cloves, sliced
2 tablespoons chopped parsley
Cooking spray

1. Select Preheat, adjust the temperature to 390°F (199°C), set time to 10 to 12 minutes and press Start/Pause. Spritz the air fryer basket with cooking spray. 2. On a plate, place the flour. In a shallow bowl, whisk the eggs with salt. In another shallow bowl, combine the bread crumbs and Italian seasoning. 3. Dredge the eggplant slices, one at a time, in the flour, then in the whisked eggs, finally in the bread crumb mixture to coat well. 4. Once preheated, arrange the coated eggplant slices in the air fryer basket and cook. Flip the eggplant slices halfway through the cooking time. It will be done until golden brown and crispy. 5. Transfer the eggplant slices to a plate and sprinkle the garlic and parsley on top before serving.

Vegetable Burgers

Prep time: 10 minutes | Cook time: 12 minutes | Serves 4

8 ounces (227 g) cremini mushrooms
2 large egg yolks
½ medium zucchini, trimmed and chopped
¼ cup peeled and chopped yellow onion

1 clove garlic, peeled and finely minced
½ teaspoon salt
¼ teaspoon ground black pepper

1. Select Preheat, adjust the temperature to 375°F (191°C), set time to 12 minutes and press Start/Pause. 2. Place all ingredients into a food processor and pulse twenty times until finely chopped and combined. 3. Separate mixture into four equal sections and press each into a burger shape. 4. Once preheated, place burgers into ungreased air fryer basket and cook, turning burgers halfway through cooking. Burgers will be browned and firm when done. Place burgers on a large plate and let cool 5 minutes before serving.

Cheesy Cabbage Wedges

Prep time: 5 minutes | Cook time: 20 minutes | Serves 4

4 tablespoons melted butter
1 head cabbage, cut into wedges
1 cup shredded Parmesan cheese

Salt and black pepper, to taste
½ cup shredded Mozzarella cheese

1. Select Preheat, adjust the temperature to 380°F (193°C), set time to 20 minutes and press Start/Pause. 2. Brush the melted butter over the cut sides of cabbage wedges and sprinkle both sides with the Parmesan cheese. Season with salt and pepper to taste. 3. Once preheated, place the cabbage wedges in the air fryer basket and cook, flipping the cabbage halfway through. It will be done until the cabbage wedges are lightly browned. 4. Transfer the cabbage wedges to a plate and serve with the Mozzarella cheese sprinkled on top.

Chapter 6   Vegetables and Sides

Bacon Potatoes and Green Beans

Prep time: 10 minutes | Cook time: 25 minutes | Serves 4

Oil, for spraying
2 pounds (907 g) medium russet potatoes, quartered
¾ cup bacon bits

10 ounces (283 g) fresh green beans
1 teaspoon salt
½ teaspoon freshly ground black pepper

1. Select Preheat, adjust the temperature to 355ºF (179ºC), set time to 25 minutes and press Start/Pause. 2. Line the air fryer basket with parchment and spray lightly with oil. Top the potatoes with the bacon bits and green beans, sprinkle with the salt and black pepper and spray liberally with oil. 3. Once preheated, place the potatoes in the prepared basket and cook, stirring after 12 minutes and spraying with oil, until the potatoes are easily pierced with a fork.

Asian Tofu Salad

Prep time: 25 minutes | Cook time: 15 minutes | Serves 2

Tofu:
1 tablespoon soy sauce
1 tablespoon vegetable oil
1 teaspoon minced fresh ginger
Salad:
¼ cup rice vinegar
1 tablespoon sugar
1 teaspoon salt
1 teaspoon black pepper
¼ cup sliced scallions

1 teaspoon minced garlic
8 ounces (227 g) extra-firm tofu, drained and cubed

1 cup julienned cucumber
1 cup julienned red onion
1 cup julienned carrots
6 butter lettuce leaves

Make the Tofu: 1. In a small bowl, whisk together the soy sauce, vegetable oil, ginger, and garlic. Add the tofu and mix gently. Let stand at room temperature for 10 minutes. 2. Select Preheat, adjust the temperature to 400ºF (204ºC), set time to 15 minutes and press Start/Pause. 3. Once preheated, arrange the tofu in the air fryer basket and cook, shaking halfway through the cooking time. Meanwhile, **Make the Salad:** 4. In a large bowl, whisk together the vinegar, sugar, salt, pepper, and scallions. Add the cucumber, onion, and carrots and toss to combine. Set aside to marinate while the tofu cooks. 5. To serve, arrange three lettuce leaves on each of two plates. Pile the marinated vegetables (and marinade) on the lettuce. Divide the tofu between the plates and serve.

Dijon Roast Cabbage

Prep time: 10 minutes | Cook time: 10 minutes | Serves 4

1 small head cabbage, cored and sliced into 1-inch-thick slices
2 tablespoons olive oil, divided
½ teaspoon salt

1 tablespoon Dijon mustard
1 teaspoon apple cider vinegar
1 teaspoon granular erythritol

1. Select Preheat, adjust the temperature to 350ºF (177ºC), set time to 10 minutes and press Start/Pause. 2. Drizzle each cabbage slice with 1 tablespoon olive oil, then sprinkle with salt. Once preheated, place slices into ungreased air fryer basket and cook, working in batches if needed. Cabbage will be tender and edges will begin to brown when done. 3. In a small bowl, whisk remaining olive oil with mustard, vinegar, and erythritol. Drizzle over cabbage in a large serving dish. Serve warm.

Dill-and-Garlic Beets

Prep time: 10 minutes | Cook time: 30 minutes | Serves 4

4 beets, cleaned, peeled, and sliced
1 garlic clove, minced
2 tablespoons chopped fresh dill

¼ teaspoon salt
¼ teaspoon black pepper
3 tablespoons olive oil

1. Select Preheat, adjust the temperature to 380°F (193°C), set time to 15 minutes and press Start/Pause. 2. In a large bowl, mix together all of the ingredients so the beets are well coated with the oil. 3. Once preheated, pour the beet mixture into the air fryer basket and cook before stirring, then continue roasting for 15 minutes more.

Buttery Mushrooms

Prep time: 10 minutes | Cook time: 10 minutes | Serves 4

8 ounces (227 g) cremini mushrooms, halved
2 tablespoons salted butter, melted

¼ teaspoon salt
¼ teaspoon ground black pepper

1. Select Preheat, adjust the temperature to 400°F (204°C), set time to 10 minutes and press Start/Pause. 2. In a medium bowl, toss mushrooms with butter, then sprinkle with salt and pepper. Once preheated, place into ungreased air fryer basket and cook, shaking the basket halfway through cooking. Mushrooms will be tender when done. Serve warm.

Parsnip Fries with Romesco Sauce

Prep time: 20 minutes | Cook time: 24 minutes | Serves 2

Romesco Sauce:
1 red bell pepper, halved and seeded
1 (1-inch) thick slice of Italian bread, torn into pieces (about 1 to 1½ cups)
1 cup almonds, toasted
Olive oil
½ Jalapeño pepper, seeded
1 tablespoon fresh parsley leaves
1 clove garlic
2 Roma tomatoes, peeled and seeded (or ⅓ cup canned

crushed tomatoes)
1 tablespoon red wine vinegar
¼ teaspoon smoked paprika
½ teaspoon salt
¾ cup olive oil
3 parsnips, peeled and cut into long strips
2 teaspoons olive oil
Salt and freshly ground black pepper, to taste

1. Select Preheat, adjust the temperature to 400°F (204°C), set time to 8 to 10 minutes and press Start/Pause. 2. Once preheated, place the red pepper halves, cut side down, in the air fryer basket and cook. It will be done until the skin turns black all over. Remove the pepper from the air fryer and let it cool. When it is cool enough to handle, peel the pepper. 3. Toss the torn bread and almonds with a little olive oil. Put in basket and cook for 4 minutes, shaking the basket a couple times throughout the cooking time. When the bread and almonds are nicely toasted, remove them from the air fryer and let them cool for just a minute or two. 4. Combine the toasted bread, almonds, roasted red pepper, Jalapeño pepper, parsley, garlic, tomatoes, vinegar, smoked paprika and salt in a food processor or blender. Process until smooth. With the processor running, add the olive oil through the feed tube until the sauce comes together in a smooth paste that is barely pourable. 5. Toss the parsnip strips with the olive oil, salt and freshly ground black pepper and cook at 400°F (204°C) for 10 minutes, shaking the basket a couple times during the cooking process so they brown and cook evenly. Serve the parsnip fries warm with the Romesco sauce to dip into.

Tingly Chili-Roasted Broccoli

Prep time: 5 minutes | Cook time: 10 minutes | Serves 2

12 ounces (340 g) broccoli florets
2 tablespoons Asian hot chili oil
1 teaspoon ground Sichuan peppercorns (or black pepper)

2 garlic cloves, finely chopped
1 (2-inch) piece fresh ginger, peeled and finely chopped
Kosher salt and freshly ground black pepper, to taste

1. Select Preheat, adjust the temperature to 375°F (191°C), set time to 10 minutes and press Start/Pause. 2. In a bowl, toss together the broccoli, chili oil, Sichuan peppercorns, garlic, ginger, and salt and black pepper to taste. 3. Once preheated, transfer to the air fryer basket and cook, shaking the basket halfway through. It will be done until lightly charred and tender. Remove from the air fryer and serve warm.

Butternut Squash Croquettes

Prep time: 5 minutes | Cook time: 17 minutes | Serves 4

⅓ butternut squash, peeled and grated
⅓ cup all-purpose flour
2 eggs, whisked
4 cloves garlic, minced
1½ tablespoons olive oil

1 teaspoon fine sea salt
⅓ teaspoon freshly ground black pepper, or more to taste
⅓ teaspoon dried sage
A pinch of ground allspice

1. Select Preheat, adjust the temperature to 345°F (174°C), set time to 17 minutes and press Start/Pause. Line the air fryer basket with parchment paper. 2. In a mixing bowl, stir together all the ingredients until well combined. **Make the Squash Croquettes:** 3. Use a small cookie scoop to drop tablespoonfuls of the squash mixture onto a lightly floured surface and shape into balls with your hands. 4. Once preheated, transfer them to the air fryer basket and cook. It will be done until the squash croquettes are golden brown. 5. Remove from the basket to a plate and serve warm.

Mushrooms with Goat Cheese

Prep time: 10 minutes | Cook time: 10 minutes | Serves 4

3 tablespoons vegetable oil
1 pound (454 g) mixed mushrooms, trimmed and sliced
1 clove garlic, minced
¼ teaspoon dried thyme

½ teaspoon black pepper
4 ounces (113 g) goat cheese, diced
2 teaspoons chopped fresh thyme leaves (optional)

1. Select Preheat, adjust the temperature to 400°F (204°C), set time to 10 minutes and press Start/Pause. 2. In a baking pan, combine the oil, mushrooms, garlic, dried thyme, and pepper. Stir in the goat cheese. Once preheated, place the pan in the air fryer basket and cook, stirring halfway through the cooking time. 3. Sprinkle with fresh thyme, if desired.

Easy Potato Croquettes

Prep time: 15 minutes | Cook time: 15 minutes | Serves 10

¼ cup nutritional yeast
2 cups boiled potatoes, mashed
1 flax egg
1 tablespoon flour

2 tablespoons chopped chives
Salt and ground black pepper, to taste
2 tablespoons vegetable oil
¼ cup bread crumbs

1. Select Preheat, adjust the temperature to 400ºF (204ºC), set time to 15 minutes and press Start/Pause. 2. In a bowl, combine the nutritional yeast, potatoes, flax egg, flour, and chives. Sprinkle with salt and pepper as desired. 3. In a separate bowl, mix the vegetable oil and bread crumbs to achieve a crumbly consistency. 4. Shape the potato mixture into small balls and dip each one into the bread crumb mixture. 5. Once preheated, put the croquettes inside the air fryer and cook, ensuring the croquettes turn golden brown. 6. Serve immediately.

Chapter 7   Family Favorites

Avocado and Egg Burrito

Prep time: 10 minutes | Cook time: 3 to 5 minutes | Serves 4

2 hard-boiled egg whites, chopped
1 hard-boiled egg, chopped
1 avocado, peeled, pitted, and chopped
1 red bell pepper, chopped
3 tablespoons low-sodium salsa, plus additional for

serving (optional)
1 (1.2-ounce / 34-g) slice low-sodium, low-fat American cheese, torn into pieces
4 low-sodium whole-wheat flour tortillas

1. Select Preheat, adjust the temperature to 390°F (199°C), set time to 3 to 5 minutes and press Start/Pause. 2. In a medium bowl, thoroughly mix the egg whites, egg, avocado, red bell pepper, salsa, and cheese. 3. Place the tortillas on a work surface and evenly divide the filling among them. Fold in the edges and roll up. Secure the burritos with toothpicks if necessary. 4. Once preheated, put the burritos in the air fryer basket and cook. It will be done until the burritos are light golden brown and crisp. Serve with more salsa (if using).

Elephant Ears

Prep time: 5 minutes | Cook time: 5 minutes | Serves 8

Oil, for spraying
1 (8-ounce / 227-g) can buttermilk biscuits
3 tablespoons sugar

1 tablespoon ground cinnamon
3 tablespoons unsalted butter, melted
8 scoops vanilla ice cream (optional)

1. Select Preheat, adjust the temperature to 350°F (177°C), set time to 5 minutes and press Start/Pause. Line the air fryer basket with parchment and spray lightly with oil. 2. Separate the dough. Using a rolling pin, roll out the biscuits into 6- to 8-inch circles. 3. Once preheated, place the dough circles in the prepared basket, spray liberally with oil and cook. You may need to work in batches, depending on the size of your air fryer. It will be done until lightly browned. 4. In a small bowl, mix together the sugar and cinnamon. 5. Brush the elephant ears with the melted butter and sprinkle with the cinnamon-sugar mixture. 6. Top each serving with a scoop of ice cream (if using).

Puffed Egg Tarts

Prep time: 10 minutes | Cook time: 42 minutes | Makes 4 tarts

Oil, for spraying
All-purpose flour, for dusting
1 (12-ounce / 340-g) sheet frozen puff pastry, thawed
¾ cup shredded Cheddar cheese, divided

4 large eggs
2 teaspoons chopped fresh parsley
Salt and freshly ground black pepper, to taste

1. Select Preheat, adjust the temperature to 390°F (199°C), set time to 10 minutes and press Start/Pause. Line the air fryer basket with parchment and spray lightly with oil. 2. Lightly dust your work surface with flour. Unfold the puff pastry and cut it into 4 equal squares. Once preheated, place 2 squares in the prepared basket and cook. 4. Remove the basket. Press the center of each tart shell with a spoon to make an indentation. 5. Sprinkle 3 tablespoons of cheese into each indentation and crack 1 egg into the center of each tart shell. 6. Cook for another 7 to 11 minutes, or until the eggs are cooked to your desired doneness. 7. Repeat with the remaining puff pastry squares, cheese, and eggs. 8. Sprinkle evenly with the parsley, and season with salt and black pepper. Serve immediately.

Fish and Vegetable Tacos

Prep time: 15 minutes | Cook time: 9 to 12 minutes | Serves 4

1 pound (454 g) white fish fillets, such as sole or cod
2 teaspoons olive oil
3 tablespoons freshly squeezed lemon juice, divided
1½ cups chopped red cabbage

1 large carrot, grated
½ cup low-sodium salsa
⅓ cup low-fat Greek yogurt
4 soft low-sodium whole-wheat tortillas

1. Select Preheat, adjust the temperature to 390°F (199°C), set time to 9 to 12 minutes and press Start/Pause. 2. Brush the fish with the olive oil and sprinkle with 1 tablespoon of lemon juice. Once preheated, place the fish in the air fryer basket and cook. It will be done until the fish just flakes when tested with a fork. 3. Meanwhile, in a medium bowl, stir together the remaining 2 tablespoons of lemon juice, the red cabbage, carrot, salsa, and yogurt. 4. When the fish is cooked, remove it from the air fryer basket and break it up into large pieces. 5. Offer the fish, tortillas, and the cabbage mixture, and let each person assemble a taco.

Steak Tips and Potatoes

Prep time: 10 minutes | Cook time: 20 minutes | Serves 4

Oil, for spraying
8 ounces (227 g) baby gold potatoes, cut in half
½ teaspoon salt
1 pound (454 g) steak, cut into ½-inch pieces

1 teaspoon Worcestershire sauce
1 teaspoon granulated garlic
½ teaspoon salt
½ teaspoon freshly ground black pepper

1. Select Preheat, adjust the temperature to 400°F (204°C), set time to 12 to 17 minutes and press Start/Pause. Line the air fryer basket with parchment and spray lightly with oil. 2. In a microwave-safe bowl, combine the potatoes and salt, then pour in about ½ inch of water. Microwave for 7 minutes, or until the potatoes are nearly tender. Drain. 3. In a large bowl, gently mix together the steak, potatoes, Worcestershire sauce, garlic, salt, and black pepper. 4. Once preheated, Spread the mixture in the preheated air fryer basket and cook, stirring after 5 to 6 minutes. The cooking time will depend on the thickness of the meat and preferred doneness.

Meatball Subs

Prep time: 15 minutes | Cook time: 19 minutes | Serves 6

Oil, for spraying
1 pound (454 g) 85% lean ground beef
½ cup Italian bread crumbs
1 tablespoon dried minced onion
1 tablespoon minced garlic
1 large egg
1 teaspoon salt

1 teaspoon freshly ground black pepper
6 hoagie rolls
1 (18-ounce / 510-g) jar marinara sauce
1½ cups shredded Mozzarella cheese

1. Select Preheat, adjust the temperature to 390°F (199°C), set time to 15 minutes and press Start/Pause. Line the air fryer basket with parchment and spray lightly with oil. 2. In a large bowl, mix together the ground beef, bread crumbs, onion, garlic, egg, salt, and black pepper. Roll the mixture into 18 meatballs. 3. Once preheated, place the meatballs in the prepared basket and cook. 4. Place 3 meatballs in each hoagie roll. Top with marinara and Mozzarella cheese. 5. Place the loaded rolls in the air fryer and cook for 3 to 4 minutes, or until the cheese is melted. You may need to work in batches, depending on the size of your air fryer. Serve immediately.

Steak and Vegetable Kebabs

Prep time: 15 minutes | Cook time: 5 to 7 minutes | Serves 4

2 tablespoons balsamic vinegar
2 teaspoons olive oil
½ teaspoon dried marjoram
⅛ teaspoon freshly ground black pepper

¾ pound (340 g) round steak, cut into 1-inch pieces
1 red bell pepper, sliced
16 button mushrooms
1 cup cherry tomatoes

1. Select Preheat, adjust the temperature to 390°F (199°C), set time to 5 to 7 minutes and press Start/Pause. 2. In a medium bowl, stir together the balsamic vinegar, olive oil, marjoram, and black pepper. 3. Add the steak and stir to coat. Let stand for 10 minutes at room temperature. 4. Alternating items, thread the beef, red bell pepper, mushrooms, and tomatoes onto 8 bamboo or metal skewers that fit in the air fryer. 5. Once preheated, place the skewers into the air fryer basket and cook. It will be done when the beef is browned and reaches at least 145°F (63°C) on a meat thermometer. Serve immediately.

Old Bay Tilapia

Prep time: 15 minutes | Cook time: 6 minutes | Serves 4

Oil, for spraying
1 cup panko bread crumbs
2 tablespoons Old Bay seasoning
2 teaspoons granulated garlic
1 teaspoon onion powder

½ teaspoon salt
¼ teaspoon freshly ground black pepper
1 large egg
4 tilapia fillets

1. Select Preheat, adjust the temperature to 400°F (204°C), set time to 4 to 6 minutes and press Start/Pause. Line the air fryer basket with parchment and spray lightly with oil. 2. In a shallow bowl, mix together the bread crumbs, Old Bay, garlic, onion powder, salt, and black pepper. 3. In a small bowl, whisk the egg. 4. Coat the tilapia in the egg, then dredge in the bread crumb mixture until completely coated. 5. Once preheated, spray lightly with oil. Place the tilapia in the prepared basket and cook. You may need to work in batches, depending on the size of your air fryer. It will be done until the internal temperature reaches 145°F (63°C), depending on the thickness of the fillets. Serve immediately.

Berry Cheesecake

Prep time: 5 minutes | Cook time: 10 minutes | Serves 4

Oil, for spraying
8 ounces (227 g) cream cheese
6 tablespoons sugar
1 tablespoon sour cream

1 large egg
½ teaspoon vanilla extract
¼ teaspoon lemon juice
½ cup fresh mixed berries

1. Select Preheat, adjust the temperature to 350°F (177°C), set time to 8 to 10 minutes and press Start/Pause. Line the air fryer basket with parchment and spray lightly with oil. 2. In a blender, combine the cream cheese, sugar, sour cream, egg, vanilla, and lemon juice and blend until smooth. Pour the mixture into a 4-inch springform pan. 3. Once preheated, place the pan in the prepared basket and cook. It will be done until only the very center jiggles slightly when the pan is moved. 4. Refrigerate the cheesecake in the pan for at least 2 hours. 5. Release the sides from the springform pan, top the cheesecake with the mixed berries, and serve.

Scallops with Green Vegetables

Prep time: 15 minutes | Cook time: 8 to 11 minutes | Serves 4

1 cup green beans
1 cup frozen peas
1 cup frozen chopped broccoli
2 teaspoons olive oil

½ teaspoon dried basil
½ teaspoon dried oregano
12 ounces (340 g) sea scallops

1. Select Preheat, adjust the temperature to 400°F (204°C), set time to 4 to 6 minutes and press Start/Pause. 2. In a large bowl, toss the green beans, peas, and broccoli with the olive oil. Once preheated, place in the air fryer basket and cook. The vegetables are crisp-tender when done. 3. Remove the vegetables from the air fryer basket and sprinkle with the herbs. Set aside. 4. In the air fryer basket, put the scallops and cook for 4 to 5 minutes, or until the scallops are firm and reach an internal temperature of just 145°F (63°C) on a meat thermometer. 5. Toss scallops with the vegetables and serve immediately.

Mixed Berry Crumble

Prep time: 10 minutes | Cook time: 11 to 16 minutes | Serves 4

½ cup chopped fresh strawberries
½ cup fresh blueberries
⅓ cup frozen raspberries
1 tablespoon freshly squeezed lemon juice

1 tablespoon honey
⅔ cup whole-wheat pastry flour
3 tablespoons packed brown sugar
2 tablespoons unsalted butter, melted

1. Select Preheat, adjust the temperature to 380°F (193°C), set time to 11 to 16 minutes and press Start/Pause. 2. In a baking pan, combine the strawberries, blueberries, and raspberries. Drizzle with the lemon juice and honey. 3. In a small bowl, mix the pastry flour and brown sugar. 4. Stir in the butter and mix until crumbly. Sprinkle this mixture over the fruit. 5. Once preheated, place the baking pan into the air fryer basket. It will be done until the fruit is tender and bubbly and the topping is golden brown. Serve warm.

Pecan Rolls

Prep time: 20 minutes | Cook time: 20 to 24 minutes | Makes 12 rolls

2 cups all-purpose flour, plus more for dusting
2 tablespoons granulated sugar, plus ¼ cup, divided
1 teaspoon salt
3 tablespoons butter, at room temperature
¾ cup milk, whole or 2%

¼ cup packed light brown sugar
½ cup chopped pecans, toasted
1 to 2 tablespoons oil
¼ cup confectioners' sugar (optional)

1. Select Preheat, adjust the temperature to 320°F (160°C), set time to 5 minutes and press Start/Pause. Line the air fryer basket with parchment paper and spritz the parchment with oil. 2. In a large bowl, whisk the flour, 2 tablespoons granulated sugar, and salt until blended. Stir in the butter and milk briefly until a sticky dough forms. 3. In a small bowl, stir together the brown sugar and remaining ¼ cup of granulated sugar. 4. Place a piece of parchment paper on a work surface and dust it with flour. Roll the dough on the prepared surface to ¼ inch thickness. 5. Spread the sugar mixture over the dough. Sprinkle the pecans on top. Roll up the dough jelly roll-style, pinching the ends to seal. Cut the dough into 12 rolls. 6. Once preheated, place 6 rolls on the prepared parchment and cook. Flip the rolls and cook for 5 to 7 minutes more until lightly browned. Repeat with the remaining rolls. 8. Sprinkle with confectioners' sugar (if using).

Churro Bites

Oil, for spraying
1 (17¼-ounce / 489-g) package frozen puffed pastry, thawed
1 cup granulated sugar

1 tablespoon ground cinnamon
½ cup confectioners' sugar
1 tablespoon milk

1. Select Preheat, adjust the temperature to 400°F (204°C), set time to 3 minutes and press Start/Pause. Line the air fryer basket with parchment and spray lightly with oil. 2. Unfold the puff pastry onto a clean work surface. Using a sharp knife, cut the dough into 36 bite-size pieces. 3. Once preheated, place the dough pieces in the prepared basket, taking care not to let the pieces touch or overlap. 4. When finished, flip, and cook for another 3 minutes, or until puffed and golden. 5. In a small bowl, mix together the granulated sugar and cinnamon. 6. In another small bowl, whisk together the confectioners' sugar and milk. 7. Dredge the bites in the cinnamon-sugar mixture until evenly coated. 8. Serve with the icing on the side for dipping.

Cheesy Roasted Sweet Potatoes

2 large sweet potatoes, peeled and sliced
1 teaspoon olive oil
1 tablespoon white balsamic vinegar

1 teaspoon dried thyme
¼ cup grated Parmesan cheese

1. Select Preheat, adjust the temperature to 400°F (204°C), set time to 18 to 23 minutes and press Start/Pause. 2. In a large bowl, drizzle the sweet potato slices with the olive oil and toss. 3. Sprinkle with the balsamic vinegar and thyme and toss again. 4. Sprinkle the potatoes with the Parmesan cheese and toss to coat. 5. Once preheated, place the potatoes in the air fryer basket and cook, working in batches. Tossing the sweet potato slices in the basket once during cooking, until tender. 6. Repeat with the remaining sweet potato slices. Serve immediately.

Veggie Tuna Melts

2 low-sodium whole-wheat English muffins, split
1 (6-ounce / 170-g) can chunk light low-sodium tuna, drained
1 cup shredded carrot
⅓ cup chopped mushrooms

2 scallions, white and green parts, sliced
⅓ cup nonfat Greek yogurt
2 tablespoons low-sodium stone-ground mustard
2 slices low-sodium low-fat Swiss cheese, halved

1. Select Preheat, adjust the temperature to 340°F (171°C), set time to 3 to 4 minutes and press Start/Pause. 2. Once preheated, place the English muffin halves in the air fryer basket. It will be done when the muffins are crisp. Remove from the basket and set aside. 3. In a medium bowl, thoroughly mix the tuna, carrot, mushrooms, scallions, yogurt, and mustard. Top each half of the muffins with one-fourth of the tuna mixture and a half slice of Swiss cheese. 4. Put in basket and cook for 4 to 7 minutes, or until the tuna mixture is hot and the cheese melts and starts to brown. Serve immediately.

Chapter 8   Holiday Specials

Mushroom and Green Bean Casserole

Prep time: 10 minutes | Cook time: 15 minutes | Serves 4

4 tablespoons unsalted butter
¼ cup diced yellow onion
½ cup chopped white mushrooms
½ cup heavy whipping cream
1 ounce (28 g) full-fat cream cheese

½ cup chicken broth
¼ teaspoon xanthan gum
1 pound (454 g) fresh green beans, edges trimmed
½ ounce (14 g) pork rinds, finely ground

1. Select Preheat, adjust the temperature to 320°F (160°C), set time to 15 minutes and press Start/Pause. 2. In a medium skillet over medium heat, melt the butter. Sauté the onion and mushrooms until they become soft and fragrant, about 3 to 5 minutes. 3. Add the heavy whipping cream, cream cheese, and broth to the pan. Whisk until smooth. Bring to a boil and then reduce to a simmer. Sprinkle the xanthan gum into the pan and remove from heat. 4. Chop the green beans into 2-inch pieces and place into a baking dish. Pour the sauce mixture over them and stir until coated. Top the dish with ground pork rinds. 5. Once preheated, put into the air fryer basket and cook. Top will be golden and green beans fork-tender when fully cooked. 6. Serve warm.

Custard Donut Holes with Chocolate Glaze

Prep time: 1 hour 50 minutes | Cook time: 4 minutes per batch | Makes 24 donut holes

Dough:
1½ cups bread flour
2 egg yolks
1 teaspoon active dry yeast
½ cup warm milk
½ teaspoon pure vanilla extract
Custard Filling:
1 (3.4-ounce / 96-g) box French vanilla instant pudding mix
¼ cup heavy cream
¾ cup whole milk
Special Equipment:
A pastry bag with a long tip

2 tablespoons butter, melted
1 tablespoon sugar
¼ teaspoon salt
Cooking spray

Chocolate Glaze:
⅓ cup heavy cream
1 cup chocolate chips

1. Combine the ingredients for the dough in a food processor, then pulse until a satiny dough ball forms. 2. Transfer the dough on a lightly floured work surface, then knead for 2 minutes by hand and shape the dough back to a ball. 3. Spritz a large bowl with cooking spray, then transfer the dough ball into the bowl. Wrap the bowl in plastic and let it rise for 1½ hours or until it doubled in size. 4. Transfer the risen dough on a floured work surface, then shape it into a 24-inch long log. Cut the log into 24 parts and shape each part into a ball. 5. Transfer the balls on two or three baking sheets and let sit to rise for 30 more minutes. 6. Select Preheat, adjust the temperature to 400°F (204°C), set time to 4 minutes and press Start/Pause. 7. Once preheated, arrange the baking sheets in the air fryer basket, spritz the balls with cooking spray and cook. You need to work in batches to avoid overcrowding. It will be done until golden brown. Flip the balls halfway through. 8. Meanwhile, combine the ingredients for the filling in a large bowl and whisk for 2 minutes with a hand mixer until well combined. 9. Pour the heavy cream in a saucepan, then bring to a boil. Put the chocolate chips in a small bowl and pour in the boiled heavy cream immediately. Mix until the chocolate chips are melted and the mixture is smooth. 10. Transfer the baked donut holes to a large plate, then pierce a hole into each donut hole and lightly hollow them. 11. Pour the filling in a pastry bag with a long tip and gently squeeze the filling into the donut holes. Then top the donut holes with chocolate glaze. 12. Allow to sit for 10 minutes, then serve.

Whole Chicken Roast

1 teaspoon salt

1 teaspoon Italian seasoning

½ teaspoon freshly ground black pepper

½ teaspoon paprika

½ teaspoon garlic powder

½ teaspoon onion powder

2 tablespoons olive oil, plus more as needed

1 (4-pound / 1.8-kg) fryer chicken

1. Select Preheat, adjust the temperature to 360°F (182°C), set time to 30 minutes and press Start/Pause. Grease the air fryer basket lightly with olive oil. 2. In a small bowl, mix the salt, Italian seasoning, pepper, paprika, garlic powder, and onion powder. 3. Remove any giblets from the chicken. Pat the chicken dry thoroughly with paper towels, including the cavity. 4. Brush the chicken all over with the olive oil and rub it with the seasoning mixture. 5. Truss the chicken or tie the legs with butcher's twine. This will make it easier to flip the chicken during cooking. 6. Once preheated, put the chicken in the air fryer basket, breast-side down, and cook. 7. When done, flip the chicken over and baste it with any drippings collected in the bottom drawer of the air fryer. Lightly brush the chicken with olive oil and cook for another 20 minutes. 8. Flip the chicken over one last time and air fry until a thermometer inserted into the thickest part of the thigh reaches at least 165°F (74°C) and it's crispy and golden, 10 more minutes. Continue to cook, checking every 5 minutes until the chicken reaches the correct internal temperature. 9. Let the chicken rest for 10 minutes before carving and serving.

Hearty Honey Yeast Rolls

¼ cup whole milk, heated to 115°F (46°C) in the microwave

½ teaspoon active dry yeast

1 tablespoon honey

⅔ cup all-purpose flour, plus more for dusting

½ teaspoon kosher salt

2 tablespoons unsalted butter, at room temperature, plus more for greasing

Flaky sea salt, to taste

1. In a large bowl, whisk together the milk, yeast, and honey and let stand until foamy, about 10 minutes. 2. Stir in the flour and salt until just combined. Stir in the butter until absorbed. Scrape the dough onto a lightly floured work surface and knead until smooth, about 6 minutes. 3. Transfer the dough to a lightly greased bowl, cover loosely with a sheet of plastic wrap or a kitchen towel, and let sit until nearly doubled in size, about 1 hour. 4. Uncover the dough, lightly press it down to expel the bubbles, then portion it into 8 equal pieces. Prep the work surface by wiping it clean with a damp paper towel (if there is flour on the work surface, it will prevent the dough from sticking lightly to the surface, which helps it form a ball). Roll each piece into a ball by cupping the palm of the hand around the dough against the work surface and moving the heel of the hand in a circular motion while using the thumb to contain the dough and tighten it into a perfectly round ball. 5. Once all the balls are formed, nestle them side by side in the air fryer basket. Cover the rolls loosely with a kitchen towel or a sheet of plastic wrap and let sit until lightly risen and puffed, 20 to 30 minutes. 6. Select Preheat, adjust the temperature to 270°F (132°C), set time to 12 minutes and press Start/Pause. 7. Once preheated, uncover the rolls and gently brush with more butter, being careful not to press the rolls too hard. The rolls will be light golden brown and fluffy when done. 7. Remove the rolls from the air fryer and brush liberally with more butter, if you like, and sprinkle each roll with a pinch of sea salt. Serve warm.

Air Fried Blistered Tomatoes

Prep time: 5 minutes | Cook time: 10 minutes | Serves 4 to 6

2 pounds (907 g) cherry tomatoes
2 tablespoons olive oil
2 teaspoons balsamic vinegar

½ teaspoon salt
½ teaspoon ground black pepper

1. Select Preheat, adjust the temperature to 400°F (204°C), set time to 10 minutes and press Start/Pause. 2. Toss the cherry tomatoes with olive oil in a large bowl to coat well. 3. Once preheated, pour the tomatoes in the cake pan and cook. Tomatoes will be blistered and lightly wilted when done. Shake the basket halfway through. 4. Transfer the blistered tomatoes to a large bowl and toss with balsamic vinegar, salt, and black pepper before serving.

Teriyaki Shrimp Skewers

Prep time: 10 minutes | Cook time: 6 minutes | Makes 12 skewered shrimp

1½ tablespoons mirin
1½ teaspoons ginger juice
1½ tablespoons soy sauce
12 large shrimp (about 20 shrimps per pound), peeled

and deveined
1 large egg
¾ cup panko breadcrumbs
Cooking spray

1. Combine the mirin, ginger juice, and soy sauce in a large bowl. Stir to mix well. 2. Dunk the shrimp in the bowl of mirin mixture, then wrap the bowl in plastic and refrigerate for 1 hour to marinate. 3. Select Preheat, adjust the temperature to 400°F (204°C), set time to 6 minutes and press Start/Pause. Spritz the air fryer basket with cooking spray. 4. Run twelve 4-inch skewers through each shrimp. 5. Whisk the egg in the bowl of marinade to combine well. Pour the breadcrumbs on a plate. 6. Dredge the shrimp skewers in the egg mixture, then shake the excess off and roll over the breadcrumbs to coat well. 7. Once preheated, arrange the shrimp skewers in the preheated air fryer basket and spritz with cooking spray. You need to work in batches to avoid overcrowding. It will be done until the shrimp are opaque and firm. Flip the shrimp skewers halfway through. 9. Serve immediately.

Golden Nuggets

Prep time: 15 minutes | Cook time: 4 minutes per batch | Makes 20 nuggets

1 cup all-purpose flour, plus more for dusting
1 teaspoon baking powder
½ teaspoon butter, at room temperature, plus more for brushing
¼ teaspoon salt

¼ cup water
⅛ teaspoon onion powder
¼ teaspoon garlic powder
⅛ teaspoon seasoning salt
Cooking spray

1. Select Preheat, adjust the temperature to 370°F (188°C), set time to 4 minutes and press Start/Pause. Line the air fryer basket with parchment paper. 2. Mix the flour, baking powder, butter, and salt in a large bowl. Stir to mix well. Gradually whisk in the water until a sanity dough forms. 3. Put the dough on a lightly floured work surface, then roll it out into a ½-inch thick rectangle with a rolling pin. 4. Once preheated, cut the dough into about twenty 1- or 2-inch squares, then arrange the squares in the preheated air fryer basket. Spritz with cooking spray and cook. You need to work in batches to avoid overcrowding. 5. The dough will be done until golden brown. Flip the squares halfway through the cooking time. 6. Combine onion powder, garlic powder, and seasoning salt in a small bowl. Stir to mix well, then sprinkle the squares with the powder mixture. 7. Remove the golden nuggets from the air fryer and brush with more butter immediately. Serve warm.

Shrimp with Sriracha and Worcestershire Sauce

Prep time: 15 minutes | Cook time: 10 minutes per batch | Serves 4

1 tablespoon Sriracha sauce

1 teaspoon Worcestershire sauce

2 tablespoons sweet chili sauce

¾ cup mayonnaise

1 egg, beaten

1 cup panko breadcrumbs

1 pound (454 g) raw shrimp, shelled and deveined, rinsed and drained

Lime wedges, for serving

Cooking spray

1. Select Preheat, adjust the temperature to 360°F (182°C), set time to 10 minutes and press Start/Pause. Spritz the air fryer basket with cooking spray. 2. Combine the Sriracha sauce, Worcestershire sauce, chili sauce, and mayo in a bowl. Stir to mix well. Reserve ⅓ cup of the mixture as the dipping sauce. 3. Combine the remaining sauce mixture with the beaten egg. Stir to mix well. Put the panko in a separate bowl. 4. Dredge the shrimp in the sauce mixture first, then into the panko. Roll the shrimp to coat well. Shake the excess off. 5. Once preheated, place the shrimp in the preheated air fryer basket, then spritz with cooking spray and cook. You may need to work in batches to avoid overcrowding. Flip the shrimp halfway through the cooking time. 6. Remove the shrimp from the air fryer and serve with reserve sauce mixture and squeeze the lime wedges over.

Fried Dill Pickles with Buttermilk Dressing

Prep time: 45 minutes | Cook time: 8 minutes | Serves 6 to 8

Buttermilk Dressing:

¼ cup buttermilk

¼ cup chopped scallions

¾ cup mayonnaise

½ cup sour cream

½ teaspoon cayenne pepper

½ teaspoon onion powder

½ teaspoon garlic powder

1 tablespoon chopped chives

2 tablespoons chopped fresh dill

Kosher salt and ground black pepper, to taste

Fried Dill Pickles:

¾ cup all-purpose flour

1 (2-pound / 907-g) jar kosher dill pickles, cut into 4 spears, drained

2½ cups panko breadcrumbs

2 eggs, beaten with 2 tablespoons water

Kosher salt and ground black pepper, to taste

Cooking spray

1. Combine the ingredients for the dressing in a bowl. Stir to mix well. 2. Wrap the bowl in plastic and refrigerate for 30 minutes or until ready to serve. 3. Select Preheat, adjust the temperature to 400°F (204°C), set time to 8 minutes and press Start/Pause. 4. Pour the flour in a bowl and sprinkle with salt and ground black pepper. Stir to mix well. Put the breadcrumbs in a separate bowl. Pour the beaten eggs in a third bowl. 5. Dredge the pickle spears in the flour, then into the eggs, and then into the panko to coat well. Shake the excess off. 6. Once preheated, arrange the pickle spears in the air fryer basket, spritz with cooking spray, and cook. Flip the pickle spears halfway through. 7. Serve the pickle spears with buttermilk dressing.

Cinnamon Rolls with Cream Glaze

Prep time: 2 hours 15 minutes | Cook time: 10 minutes | Serves 8

1 pound (454 g) frozen bread dough, thawed

2 tablespoons melted butter

1½ tablespoons cinnamon

¾ cup brown sugar

Cooking spray

Cream Glaze:

4 ounces (113 g) softened cream cheese

½ teaspoon vanilla extract

2 tablespoons melted butter

1¼ cups powdered erythritol

1. Place the bread dough on a clean work surface, then roll the dough out into a rectangle with a rolling pin. 2. Brush the top of the dough with melted butter and leave 1-inch edges uncovered. 3. Combine the cinnamon and sugar in a small bowl, then sprinkle the dough with the cinnamon mixture. 4. Roll the dough over tightly, then cut the dough log into 8 portions. Wrap the portions in plastic, better separately, and let sit to rise for 1 or 2 hours. 5. Meanwhile, combine the ingredients for the glaze in a separate small bowl. Stir to mix well. 6. Select Preheat, adjust the temperature to 350ºF (177ºC), set time to 5 minutes and press Start/Pause. Spritz the air fryer basket with cooking spray. 7. Once preheated, transfer the risen rolls to the air fryer basket and cook. You may need to work in batches to avoid overcrowding. It will be done until golden brown. Flip the rolls halfway through. 8. Serve the rolls with the glaze.

Classic Churros

Prep time: 35 minutes | Cook time: 10 minutes per batch | Makes 12 churros

4 tablespoons butter

¼ teaspoon salt

½ cup water

½ cup all-purpose flour

2 large eggs

2 teaspoons ground cinnamon

¼ cup granulated white sugar

Cooking spray

1. Put the butter, salt, and water in a saucepan. Bring to a boil until the butter is melted on high heat. Keep stirring. 2. Reduce the heat to medium and fold in the flour to form a dough. Keep cooking and stirring until the dough is dried out and coat the pan with a crust. 3. Turn off the heat and scrape the dough in a large bowl. Allow to cool for 15 minutes. 4. Break and whisk the eggs into the dough with a hand mixer until the dough is sanity and firm enough to shape. 5. Scoop up 1 tablespoon of the dough and roll it into a ½-inch-diameter and 2-inch-long cylinder. Repeat with remaining dough to make 12 cylinders in total. 6. Combine the cinnamon and sugar in a large bowl and dunk the cylinders into the cinnamon mix to coat. 7. Arrange the cylinders on a plate and refrigerate for 20 minutes. 8. Select Preheat, adjust the temperature to 375ºF (191ºC), set time to 10 minutes and press Start/Pause. Spritz the air fryer basket with cooking spray. 9. Once preheated, place the cylinders in batches in the air fryer basket, spritz with cooking spray, and cook. It will be done until golden brown and fluffy. Flip them halfway through. 11. Serve immediately.

Eggnog Bread

1 cup flour, plus more for dusting

¼ cup sugar

1 teaspoon baking powder

¼ teaspoon salt

¼ teaspoon nutmeg

½ cup eggnog

1 egg yolk

1 tablespoon plus 1 teaspoon butter, melted

¼ cup pecans

¼ cup chopped candied fruit (cherries, pineapple, or mixed fruits)

Cooking spray

1. Select Preheat, adjust the temperature to 360°F (182°C), set time to 18 minutes and press Start/Pause. 2. In a medium bowl, stir together the flour, sugar, baking powder, salt, and nutmeg. 3. Add eggnog, egg yolk, and butter. Mix well but do not beat. Stir in nuts and fruit. 4. Spray a baking pan with cooking spray and dust with flour. 5. Once preheated, spread batter into prepared pan. Place the pan into the air fryer basket, and cook. It will be done when top is dark golden brown and bread starts to pull away from sides of pan. 6. Serve immediately.

Arancini

⅔ cup raw white Arborio rice

2 teaspoons butter

½ teaspoon salt

1⅓ cups water

2 large eggs, well beaten

1¼ cups seasoned Italian-style dried breadcrumbs

10 ¾-inch semi-firm Mozzarella cubes

Cooking spray

1. Pour the rice, butter, salt, and water in a pot. Stir to mix well and bring a boil over medium-high heat. Keep stirring. 2. Reduce the heat to low and cover the pot. Simmer for 20 minutes or until the rice is tender. 3. Turn off the heat and let sit, covered, for 10 minutes, then open the lid and fluffy the rice with a fork. Allow to cool for 10 more minutes. 4. Select Preheat, adjust the temperature to 375°F (191°C), set time to 10 minutes and press Start/Pause. 5. Pour the beaten eggs in a bowl, then pour the breadcrumbs in a separate bowl. 6. Scoop 2 tablespoons of the cooked rice up and form it into a ball, then press the Mozzarella into the ball and wrap. 7. Dredge the ball in the eggs first, then shake the excess off the dunk the ball in the breadcrumbs. Roll to coat evenly. Repeat to make 10 balls in total with remaining rice. 8. Once preheated, transfer the balls in the preheated air fryer basket, spritz with cooking spray, and cook. You need to work in batches to avoid overcrowding. The balls will be lightly browned and crispy when done. 9. Remove the balls from the air fryer and allow to cool before serving.

Air Fried Spicy Olives

Prep time: 10 minutes | Cook time: 5 minutes | Serves 4

12 ounces (340 g) pitted black extra-large olives
¼ cup all-purpose flour
1 cup panko bread crumbs
2 teaspoons dried thyme

1 teaspoon red pepper flakes
1 teaspoon smoked paprika
1 egg beaten with 1 tablespoon water
Vegetable oil for spraying

1. Select Preheat, adjust the temperature to 400°F (204°C), set time to 5 minutes and press Start/Pause. 2. Drain the olives and place them on a paper towel–lined plate to dry. 3. Put the flour on a plate. Combine the panko, thyme, red pepper flakes, and paprika on a separate plate. Dip an olive in the flour, shaking off any excess, then coat with egg mixture. Dredge the olive in the panko mixture, pressing to make the crumbs adhere, and place the breaded olive on a platter. Repeat with the remaining olives. 4. Once preheated, spray the olives with oil, place them in the air fryer basket and cook. Work in batches if necessary so as not to overcrowd the basket. It will be done until the breading is browned and crispy. Serve warm

Supplì al Telefono (Risotto Croquettes)

Prep time: 1 hour 40 minutes | Cook time: 1 hour | Serves 6

Risotto Croquettes:
4 tablespoons unsalted butter
1 small yellow onion, minced
1 cup Arborio rice
3½ cups chicken stock
½ cup dry white wine
3 eggs
Zest of 1 lemon
½ cup grated Parmesan cheese
Tomato Sauce:
2 tablespoons extra-virgin olive oil
4 cloves garlic, minced
¼ teaspoon red pepper flakes

2 ounces (57 g) fresh Mozzarella cheese
¼ cup peas
2 tablespoons water
½ cup all-purpose flour
1½ cups panko breadcrumbs
Kosher salt and ground black pepper, to taste
Cooking spray

1 (28-ounce / 794-g) can crushed tomatoes
2 teaspoons granulated sugar
Kosher salt and ground black pepper, to taste

1. Melt the butter in a pot over medium heat, then add the onion and salt to taste. Sauté for 5 minutes or until the onion in translucent. 2. Add the rice and stir to coat well. Cook for 3 minutes or until the rice is lightly browned. Pour in the chicken stock and wine. 3. Bring to a boil. Then cook for 20 minutes or until the rice is tender and liquid is almost absorbed. **Make the Risotto:** 4. When the rice is cooked, break the egg into the pot. Add the lemon zest and Parmesan cheese. Sprinkle with salt and ground black pepper. Stir to mix well. 5. Pour the risotto in a baking sheet, then level with a spatula to spread the risotto evenly. Wrap the baking sheet in plastic and refrigerate for1 hour. 6. Meanwhile, heat the olive oil in a saucepan over medium heat until shimmering. 7. Add the garlic and sprinkle with red pepper flakes. Sauté for a minute or until fragrant. 8. Add the crushed tomatoes and sprinkle with sugar. Stir to mix well. Bring to a boil. Reduce the heat to low and simmer for 15 minutes or until lightly thickened. Sprinkle with salt and pepper to taste. Set aside until ready to serve. 9. Remove the risotto from the refrigerator. Scoop the risotto into twelve 2-inch balls, then flatten the balls with your hands. 10. Arrange a about ½-inch piece of Mozzarella and 5 peas in the center of each flattened ball, then wrap them back into balls. 11. Transfer the balls in a baking sheet lined with parchment paper, then refrigerate for 15 minutes or until firm. 12. Select Preheat, adjust the temperature to 400°F (204°C), set time to 10 minutes and press Start/Pause. 13. Whisk the remaining 2 eggs with 2 tablespoons of water in a bowl. Pour the flour in a second bowl and pour the panko in a third bowl. 14. Dredge the risotto balls in the bowl of flour first, then into the eggs, and then into the panko. Shake the excess off. 15. Once preheated, transfer the balls in the preheated air fryer basket, spritz with cooking spray and cook. You may need to work in batches to avoid overcrowding. It will be done until golden brown. Flip the balls halfway through. 16. Serve the risotto balls with the tomato sauce.

Chapter 9 Desserts

Pecan Brownies

½ cup blanched finely ground almond flour
½ cup powdered erythritol
2 tablespoons unsweetened cocoa powder
½ teaspoon baking powder

¼ cup unsalted butter, softened
1 large egg
¼ cup chopped pecans
¼ cup low-carb, sugar-free chocolate chips

1. Select Preheat, adjust the temperature to 300°F (149°C), set time to 20 minutes and press Start/Pause. 2. In a large bowl, mix almond flour, erythritol, cocoa powder, and baking powder. Stir in butter and egg. 3. Fold in pecans and chocolate chips. Scoop mixture into a round baking pan. Once preheated, place pan into the air fryer basket and cook. 4. When fully cooked a toothpick inserted in center will come out clean. Allow 20 minutes to fully cool and firm up.

Peanut Butter-Honey-Banana Toast

2 tablespoons butter, softened
4 slices white bread
4 tablespoons peanut butter

2 bananas, peeled and thinly sliced
4 tablespoons honey
1 teaspoon ground cinnamon

1. Select Preheat, adjust the temperature to 375°F (191°C), set time to 5 minutes and press Start/Pause. 2. Spread butter on one side of each slice of bread, then peanut butter on the other side. Arrange the banana slices on top of the peanut butter sides of each slice (about 9 slices per toast). Drizzle honey on top of the banana and sprinkle with cinnamon. 3. Cut each slice in half lengthwise so that it will better fit into the air fryer basket. Once preheated, arrange two pieces of bread, butter sides down, in the air fryer basket and cook. 4. When, done, then adjust the temperature to 400°F (204°C) for an additional 4 minutes, or until the bananas have started to brown. Repeat with remaining slices. Serve hot.

Chocolate and Rum Cupcakes

¾ cup granulated erythritol
1¼ cups almond flour
1 teaspoon unsweetened baking powder
3 teaspoons cocoa powder
½ teaspoon baking soda
½ teaspoon ground cinnamon
¼ teaspoon grated nutmeg

⅛ teaspoon salt
½ cup milk
1 stick butter, at room temperature
3 eggs, whisked
1 teaspoon pure rum extract
½ cup blueberries
Cooking spray

1. Select Preheat, adjust the temperature to 345°F (174°C), set time to 15 minutes and press Start/Pause. Spray a 6-cup muffin tin with cooking spray. 2. In a mixing bowl, combine the erythritol, almond flour, baking powder, cocoa powder, baking soda, cinnamon, nutmeg, and salt and stir until well blended. 3. In another mixing bowl, mix together the milk, butter, egg, and rum extract until thoroughly combined. Slowly and carefully pour this mixture into the bowl of dry mixture. Stir in the blueberries. 4. Spoon the batter into the greased muffin cups, filling each about three-quarters full. 5. Once preheated, place the muffin cups into the air fryer basket and cook. It will be done until the center is springy and a toothpick inserted in the middle comes out clean. 6. Remove from the basket and place on a wire rack to cool. Serve immediately.

Lemon Curd Pavlova

Prep time: 10 minutes | Cook time: 1 hour | Serves 4

Shell:

3 large egg whites

¼ teaspoon cream of tartar

¾ cup Swerve confectioners'-style sweetener or

Lemon Curd:

1 cup Swerve confectioners'-style sweetener or equivalent amount of liquid or powdered sweetener

½ cup lemon juice

4 large eggs

½ cup coconut oil

equivalent amount of powdered sweetener

1 teaspoon grated lemon zest

1 teaspoon lemon extract

For Garnish (Optional):

Blueberries

Swerve confectioners'-style sweetener or equivalent amount of powdered sweetener

1. Select Preheat, adjust the temperature to 275ºF (135ºC), set time to 60 minutes and press Start/Pause. Thoroughly grease a pie pan with butter or coconut oil. **Make the Shell:** 2. In a small bowl, use a hand mixer to beat the egg whites and cream of tartar until soft peaks form. With the mixer on low, slowly sprinkle in the sweetener and mix until it's completely incorporated. 3. Add the lemon zest and lemon extract and continue to beat with the hand mixer until stiff peaks form. 4. Spoon the mixture into the greased pie pan, then smooth it across the bottom, up the sides, and onto the rim to form a shell. 5. Once preheated, place the pan into the air fryer basket and cook. When done, turn off the air fryer and let the shell stand in the air fryer for 20 minutes. (The shell can be made up to 3 days ahead and stored in an airtight container in the refrigerator, if desired.) **Make the Lemon Curd:** 6. While the shell bakes, whisk together the sweetener, lemon juice, and eggs in a medium-sized heavy-bottomed saucepan. Add the coconut oil and place the pan on the stovetop over medium heat. Once the oil is melted, whisk constantly until the mixture thickens and thickly coats the back of a spoon, about 10 minutes. Do not allow the mixture to come to a boil. 7. Pour the lemon curd mixture through a fine-mesh strainer into a medium-sized bowl. Place the bowl inside a larger bowl filled with ice water and whisk occasionally until the curd is completely cool, about 15 minutes. 8. Place the lemon curd on top of the shell and garnish with blueberries and powdered sweetener, if desired. Store leftovers in the refrigerator for up to 4 days.

Oatmeal Raisin Bars

Prep time: 15 minutes | Cook time: 15 minutes | Serves 8

⅓ cup all-purpose flour

¼ teaspoon kosher salt

¼ teaspoon baking powder

¼ teaspoon ground cinnamon

¼ cup light brown sugar, lightly packed

¼ cup granulated sugar

½ cup canola oil

1 large egg

1 teaspoon vanilla extract

1⅓ cups quick-cooking oats

⅓ cup raisins

1. Select Preheat, adjust the temperature to 360ºF (182ºC), set time to 15 minutes and press Start/Pause. 2. In a large bowl, combine the all-purpose flour, kosher salt, baking powder, ground cinnamon, light brown sugar, granulated sugar, canola oil, egg, vanilla extract, quick-cooking oats, and raisins. 3. Spray a baking pan with nonstick cooking spray, then pour the oat mixture into the pan and press down to evenly distribute. 4. Once preheated, place the pan in the air fryer basket and cook. It will be done until golden brown. 5. Remove from the air fryer and allow to cool in the pan on a wire rack for 20 minutes before slicing and serving.

Baked Apples and Walnuts

Prep time: 6 minutes | Cook time: 20 minutes | Serves 4

4 small Granny Smith apples
⅓ cup chopped walnuts
¼ cup light brown sugar
2 tablespoons butter, melted

1 teaspoon ground cinnamon
½ teaspoon ground nutmeg
½ cup water, or apple juice

1. Select Preheat, adjust the temperature to 350ºF (177ºC), set time to 20 minutes and press Start/Pause. 2. Cut off the top third of the apples. Spoon out the core and some of the flesh and discard. Place the apples in a small air fryer baking pan. 3. In a small bowl, stir together the walnuts, brown sugar, melted butter, cinnamon, and nutmeg. Spoon this mixture into the centers of the hollowed-out apples. 4. Once preheated, place the baking pan into the basket and cook. 5. When the cooking is complete, the apples should be bubbly and fork-tender.

Lemon Bars

Prep time: 15 minutes | Cook time: 25 minutes | Serves 6

¾ cup whole-wheat pastry flour
2 tablespoons confectioners' sugar
¼ cup butter, melted
½ cup granulated sugar
1 tablespoon packed grated lemon zest
¼ cup freshly squeezed lemon juice

⅛ teaspoon sea salt
¼ cup unsweetened plain applesauce
2 teaspoons cornstarch
¾ teaspoon baking powder
Cooking oil spray (sunflower, safflower, or refined coconut)

1. Select Preheat, adjust the temperature to 350ºF (177ºC), set time to 25 minutes and press Start/Pause. 2. In a small bowl, stir together the flour, confectioners' sugar, and melted butter just until well combined. Place in the refrigerator. 3. In a medium bowl, stir together the granulated sugar, lemon zest and juice, salt, applesauce, cornstarch, and baking powder. 4. Spray a round baking pan lightly with cooking oil. Remove the crust mixture from the refrigerator and gently press it into the bottom of the prepared pan . 5. Once preheated, place the pan into the basket and cook. 6. After 5 minutes, check the crust. It should be slightly firm to the touch. Remove the pan and spread the lemon filling over the crust. Reinsert the pan into the basket and resume baking for 18 to 20 minutes, or until the top is nicely browned. 7. When baking is complete, let cool for 30 minutes. Refrigerate to cool completely. Cut into pieces and serve.

Almond Shortbread

Prep time: 10 minutes | Cook time: 12 minutes | Serves 8

½ cup (1 stick) unsalted butter
½ cup sugar

1 teaspoon pure almond extract
1 cup all-purpose flour

1. Select Preheat, adjust the temperature to 375ºF (191ºC), set time to 12 minutes and press Start/Pause. 2. In bowl of a stand mixer fitted with the paddle attachment, beat the butter and sugar on medium speed until light and fluffy, 3 to 4 minutes. Add the almond extract and beat until combined, about 30 seconds. Turn the mixer to low. Add the flour a little at a time and beat for about 2 minutes more until well-incorporated. 3. Pat the dough into an even layer in a baking pan. Once preheated, place the pan in the air fryer basket And cook. 4. Carefully remove the pan from air fryer basket. While the shortbread is still warm and soft, cut it into 8 wedges. 5. Let cool in the pan on a wire rack for 5 minutes. Remove the wedges from the pan and let cool completely on the rack before serving.

Spiced Apple Cake

Prep time: 15 minutes | Cook time: 30 minutes | Serves 6

Vegetable oil
2 cups diced peeled Gala apples (about 2 apples)
1 tablespoon fresh lemon juice
¼ cup (½ stick) unsalted butter, softened
⅓ cup granulated sugar
2 large eggs
1¼ cups unbleached all-purpose flour
1½ teaspoons baking powder

1 tablespoon apple pie spice
½ teaspoon ground ginger
¼ teaspoon ground cardamom
¼ teaspoon ground nutmeg
½ teaspoon kosher salt
¼ cup whole milk
Confectioners' sugar, for dusting

1. Select Preheat, adjust the temperature to 350°F (177°C), set time to 30 minutes and press Start/Pause. Grease a 3-cup Bundt pan with oil; set aside. 2. In a medium bowl, toss the apples with the lemon juice until well coated; set aside. 3. In a large bowl, combine the butter and sugar. Beat with an electric hand mixer on medium speed until the sugar has dissolved. Add the eggs and beat until fluffy. Add the flour, baking powder, apple pie spice, ginger, cardamom, nutmeg, salt, and milk. Mix until the batter is thick but pourable. 4. Once preheated, pour the batter into the prepared pan. Top batter evenly with the apple mixture. Place the pan in the air fryer basket and cook. It will be done when a toothpick inserted in the center of the cake comes out clean. Close the air fryer and let the cake rest for 10 minutes. Turn the cake out onto a wire rack and cool completely. 5. Right before serving, dust the cake with confectioners' sugar.

Conclusion

In conclusion, you must understand that the Cosori Air Fryer is a special kitchen equipment that does special functions. If you really want to get amazing, healthy and sumptuous meal, you must take your time to understand how it works. You must also know how to take good care of your Cosori Air Fryer.

Appendix 1: Measurement Conversion Chart

VOLUME EQUIVALENTS(DRY)

US STANDARD	METRIC (APPROXIMATE)
1/8 teaspoon	0.5 mL
1/4 teaspoon	1 mL
1/2 teaspoon	2 mL
3/4 teaspoon	4 mL
1 teaspoon	5 mL
1 tablespoon	15 mL
1/4 cup	59 mL
1/2 cup	118 mL
3/4 cup	177 mL
1 cup	235 mL
2 cups	475 mL
3 cups	700 mL
4 cups	1 L

VOLUME EQUIVALENTS(LIQUID)

US STANDARD	US STANDARD (OUNCES)	METRIC (APPROXIMATE)
2 tablespoons	1 fl.oz.	30 mL
1/4 cup	2 fl.oz.	60 mL
1/2 cup	4 fl.oz.	120 mL
1 cup	8 fl.oz.	240 mL
1 1/2 cup	12 fl.oz.	355 mL
2 cups or 1 pint	16 fl.oz.	475 mL
4 cups or 1 quart	32 fl.oz.	1 L
1 gallon	128 fl.oz.	4 L

WEIGHT EQUIVALENTS

US STANDARD	METRIC (APPROXIMATE)
1 ounce	28 g
2 ounces	57 g
5 ounces	142 g
10 ounces	284 g
15 ounces	425 g
16 ounces (1 pound)	455 g
1.5 pounds	680 g
2 pounds	907 g

TEMPERATURES EQUIVALENTS

FAHRENHEIT(F)	CELSIUS(C) (APPROXIMATE)
225 °F	107 °C
250 °F	120 °C
275 °F	135 °C
300 °F	150 °C
325 °F	160 °C
350 °F	180 °C
375 °F	190 °C
400 °F	205 °C
425 °F	220 °C
450 °F	235 °C
475 °F	245 °C
500 °F	260 °C

Appendix 2:Air Fryer Cooking Chart

Beef

Item	Temp (°F)	Time (mins)	Item	Temp (°F)	Time (mins)
Beef Eye Round Roast (4 lbs.)	400 °F	45 to 55	Meatballs (1-inch)	370 °F	7
Burger Patty (4 oz.)	370 °F	16 to 20	Meatballs (3-inch)	380 °F	10
Filet Mignon (8 oz.)	400 °F	18	Ribeye, bone-in (1-inch, 8 oz)	400 °F	10 to 15
Flank Steak (1.5 lbs.)	400 °F	12	Sirloin steaks (1-inch, 12 oz)	400 °F	9 to 14
Flank Steak (2 lbs.)	400 °F	20 to 28			

Chicken

Item	Temp (°F)	Time (mins)	Item	Temp (°F)	Time (mins)
Breasts, bone in (1 ¼ lb.)	370 °F	25	Legs, bone-in (1 ¾ lb.)	380 °F	30
Breasts, boneless (4 oz)	380 °F	12	Thighs, boneless (1 ½ lb.)	380 °F	18 to 20
Drumsticks (2 ½ lb.)	370 °F	20	Wings (2 lb.)	400 °F	12
Game Hen (halved 2 lb.)	390 °F	20	Whole Chicken	360 °F	75
Thighs, bone-in (2 lb.)	380 °F	22	Tenders	360 °F	8 to 10

Pork & Lamb

Item	Temp (°F)	Time (mins)	Item	Temp (°F)	Time (mins)
Bacon (regular)	400 °F	5 to 7	Pork Tenderloin	370 °F	15
Bacon (thick cut)	400 °F	6 to 10	Sausages	380 °F	15
Pork Loin (2 lb.)	360 °F	55	Lamb Loin Chops (1-inch thick)	400 °F	8 to 12
Pork Chops, bone in (1-inch, 6.5 oz)	400 °F	12	Rack of Lamb (1.5 – 2 lb.)	380 °F	22

Fish & Seafood

Item	Temp (°F)	Time (mins)	Item	Temp (°F)	Time (mins)
Calamari (8 oz)	400 °F	4	Tuna Steak	400 °F	7 to 10
Fish Fillet (1-inch, 8 oz)	400 °F	10	Scallops	400 °F	5 to 7
Salmon, fillet (6 oz)	380 °F	12	Shrimp	400 °F	5
Swordfish steak	400 °F	10			

Appendix 3:Air Fryer Cooking Chart

Vegetables

INGREDIENT	AMOUNT	PREPARATION	OIL	TEMP	COOK TIME
Asparagus	2 bunches	Cut in half, trim stems	2 Tbsp	420°F	12-15 mins
Beets	1½ lbs	Peel, cut in ½-inch cubes	1Tbsp	390°F	28-30 mins
Bell peppers (for roasting)	4 peppers	Cut in quarters, remove seeds	1Tbsp	400°F	15-20 mins
Broccoli	1 large head	Cut in 1-2-inch florets	1Tbsp	400°F	15-20 mins
Brussels sprouts	1lb	Cut in half, remove stems	1Tbsp	425°F	15-20 mins
Carrots	1lb	Peel, cut in ¼-inch rounds	1 Tbsp	425°F	10-15 mins
Cauliflower	1 head	Cut in 1-2-inch florets	2 Tbsp	400°F	20-22 mins
Corn on the cob	7 ears	Whole ears, remove husks	1 Tbps	400°F	14-17 mins
Green beans	1 bag (12 oz)	Trim	1 Tbps	420°F	18-20 mins
Kale (for chips)	4 oz	Tear into pieces,remove stems	None	325°F	5-8 mins
Mushrooms	16 oz	Rinse, slice thinly	1 Tbps	390°F	25-30 mins
Potatoes, russet	1½ lbs	Cut in 1-inch wedges	1 Tbps	390°F	25-30 mins
Potatoes, russet	1lb	Hand-cut fries, soak 30 mins in cold water, then pat dry	½ -3 Tbps	400°F	25-28 mins
Potatoes, sweet	1lb	Hand-cut fries, soak 30 mins in cold water, then pat dry	1 Tbps	400°F	25-28 mins
Zucchini	1lb	Cut in eighths lengthwise, then cut in half	1 Tbps	400°F	15-20 mins

Printed in Great Britain
by Amazon

85887718R00059